D BROWNS

'71-402

My greatest challenge.

e Coach;
Warfield,

er, Vince
nte, Bob

Morrow,

Clark, Frank Parker, Johnny Brewer, Milt Morin, Frank Ryan.

MY
GREATEST
CHALLENGE

Bill Glass
Browns #80

MY GREATEST CHALLENGE

By

Bill Glass

WORD BOOKS, Publishers
Waco, Texas—London, England

To my beloved wife Mavis. Who for twelve years has lived and faced every play of every game with me, so that "My Greatest Challenge" has also been hers.

A WORD OF APPRECIATION . . .

To my teammates and coaches who have lived these years with me and have made them as happy and exciting as they were challenging.

To Floyd Thatcher, Senior Editor of Word Books, for his help and suggestions on the manuscript. Equal thanks to Dr. Leslie Moser for some early organizational help.

Contents

Part 1
Motivation to Face the Challenge

1

Mad Dog

"He played like a mad dog."

"He was wild-eyed and almost frothing at the mouth."

These were just two of the more colorful comments made in describing Ray Nitschke on a postgame show following the 1967 championship game between the Green Bay Packers and the Dallas Cowboys. Ray has always been known as a sort of wild man in professional football circles, and he lived up to his reputation with a vengeance in that rough bone-crusher of a game. It takes that kind of rabid dedication to be a success.

Frankly, I wouldn't like to be compared to a mad dog (I don't think Ray would either), but I do want to play every second of the game in a dedicated, intense, and gutsy way. Every game must be played as if it were for the championship—every play is crucial. As a defensive end, my job is to play hard, to hit the opposition with everything I have, to make tackles on the running game, and to clobber the quarterback every time I can crash through to him. In short, I want desperately to play a hard, intense, winning game.

A sportswriter was talking with me one day about the possible effect that being a Christian had on my ability to play football. He told me this story: "There was a player I knew who was great during his junior year in college. Then he got involved in this Christianity bit during his senior year and he seemed to go soft. I guess he just got to feeling sorry for the opposition, and he couldn't get in there and hit."

"Christ had nothing to do with this kid's sloppy showing," I answered. "He missed the best chance he'll ever have to show the world what Christianity is like. I'm sure that this kid has lost his influence with his coaches and teammates as well as the fans. Who's going to pay any attention to what a half-hearted player does or says? People, and especially young people, are interested in winners; they have no admiration for losers."

Motivation for football

Actually, being a Christian is a powerful motivation to my football career. Giving my best—making the supreme effort on every play, regardless of how much it may hurt—is an absolute must; otherwise I have no reason to play, because my influence would be diluted.

True, people can be won to Christ without my influence. He is not limited to what Bill Glass does or does not do. However, Christ has chosen to work through people to reach others, and I believe he has given me abilities as a professional football player so that I can be a witness and influence in and through the exciting sports world. In fact, the Fellowship of Christian Athletes is made up of professional and amateur athletes from all over America who are keenly aware of the frightening responsibility of their influence on people.

I thought he was dead

As much as I love football, I've had my bad moments on the field when I wondered if it was really worth it. I'll never forget one particular game with the Atlanta Falcons during the 1966 season. Their rookie quarterback, Randy Johnson, was playing a fairly good game, but he was taking a beating. We were either two or three touchdowns ahead.

On one play I faked inside, made a quick move, and was around the outside of the tackle. The quarterback was a good ten yards down the line of scrimmage with his back to me. I built up a real head of steam, watching his throwing arm as I charged toward him. His arm was cocked, but he kept hesitating. He was still looking in the other direction when my helmet crashed into the middle of his back. His neck popped, and his back bent backward the wrong way. I didn't even look to see where the ball went, although I learned later that he fumbled and we recovered —I was intent on this young kid on the ground, fearful that I had broken his back.

For a moment football wasn't important

Bending over him, I asked if he was all right, but he was unconscious. As they carried him off the field, I was sick at my stomach. A rough brand of football was one thing, but I didn't want to maim someone for life. At that moment I felt like giving up the game. A few minutes later when I glanced over toward the sideline and saw Randy walking around without any help, I was really relieved.

* * * * * * * *

My father-in-law has a ranch in South Texas, and we often go down there to hunt for deer. On this particular occasion I had been hunting all day with my two sons and my father-in-law. We had flushed out a lot of deer, but none of them had horns.

With about twenty minutes of daylight left, my seven-year-old son Bobby and I spotted several deer in the distance. One of them looked like a buck. We couldn't make out the horns at first, but they showed up through the field glasses. Just as I brought my gun up to shoot, he stepped back into the trees. "Well, Bobby, we lost our chance," I muttered with disappointment.

Suddenly, he reappeared, and trembling with anticipation, I fixed the cross hairs of my scope sight right behind his shoulder and squeezed the trigger. Pow! The buck jerked and slumped to the ground. Bobby and I yelled with excitement and scrambled down out of the blind. We covered that hundred yards or so in record time. But we stopped short as we got a closer look. My shot had found its mark, but he wasn't quite dead. There he lay —body heaving and legs kicking grotesquely in the air. He looked up at us with eyes that seemed to plead for help. What a beautiful animal! So sleek and glossy—so supple and splendidly built. The buck had been feeding, and a piece of green food still jutted from the corner of his mouth. He had been so full of life, but my bullet had changed all of that.

A wave of sadness seemed to engulf both Bobby and me as we hung the deer in a tree and prepared to clean it. In fact, I felt sick, and my stomach was tied in knots. And it was this same feeling that closed in on me as I bent over Randy Johnson.

*   *   *   *   *   *   *   *

In the dressing room after the game an Atlanta sportswriter questioned me about Randy and my reactions. I assured him that it was my job to hit hard and that I would play just as hard in the future, but I didn't want to hurt anyone—it's a rough game, and I certainly couldn't afford to let up on a quarterback.

A few days later I received the following letter:

> Dear Bill:
>   I would like to tell you how much I admire you and the work you are doing. Most people think of a big, hard-knocking player like yourself as being a rough guy who goes out every night and gets drunk. I saw you play this year down in Atlanta, and there's one thing I would like to know—what were you saying to Randy Johnson just after you lowered the boom on him? I sure felt sorry for Randy. But to see you kneel on the ground beside him and pat him

on the shoulder did me a lot of good. And the people around me all felt the same way.

Believe me, after playing four sports in high school and trying to live a Christian life, it's mighty nice to be able to say: "That Bill Glass is an All-Pro End and a good Christian. . . ."

There were no complaints from either my coaches or teammates over my concern for Randy. Actually, I'm sure they were as worried as I was. We have "class" people with the Browns. We're in the football business to win, but we have no desire to injure an opponent.

Under the same circumstances, though, I'd hit just as hard again, because the name of the game is HIT.

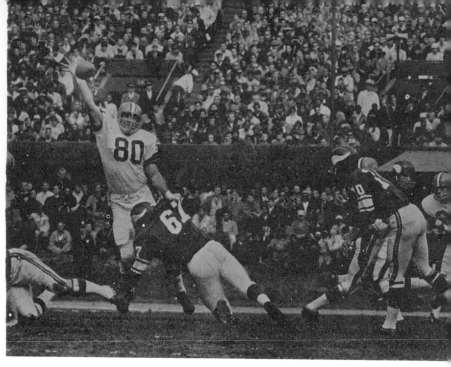

Bill Glass attempting to bat down a pass against the Minnesota Vikings.

Bill Glass tackling Timmy Brown of the Philadelphia Eagles.

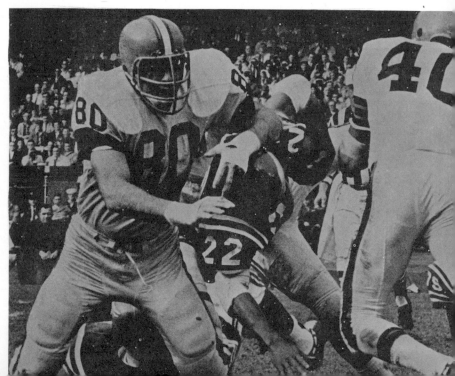

Glass stalking the greatest scrambler in the history of pro football—Fran Tarkenton.

Glass rushing the passer against the Pittsburgh Steelers—it is difficult to pass over a big lineman.

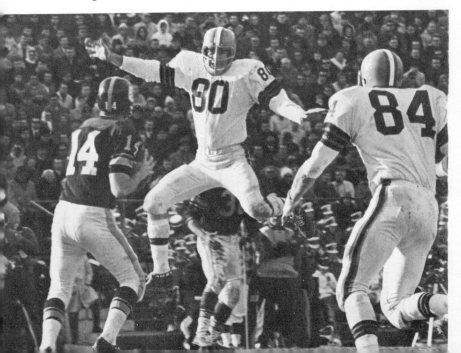

2

Action and Reaction Under Pressure

The second Dallas game of 1966 will always stand out in my mind. The stadium was packed, because this was one of the most important games of the year for both the Browns and the Cowboys. We were both still contenders for the title. Every man on the team was thinking, "This is the biggest game of the year for us; if we can beat them we will go on to the championship game of the National Football League. If we can win this one, then on to the Super Bowl!"

We were anxious to beat Dallas so we could get another crack at Green Bay. They had humiliated us the year before in the mud of the championship game. We were confident that we could take Green Bay this time, and we'd have the chance if we could only beat Dallas! I knew I was not at my best. Four days earlier we had beaten Washington, but that had been a bad day for me. I had sprained my ankle—my first serious injury in pro football. I pampered it for four days with every possible treatment the trainer and doctor could suggest. We had applied ice daily and injected cortisone into the joint. Before the game they shot it with Novocaine and deadened it from the knee down.

My ankle killed my play

The game started and I began to fire off the line into Jim Boeke, the tackle who played directly over me. Sure enough my ankle popped, but it was so numb from the Novocaine that I couldn't feel a thing. I just couldn't get any real drive off of it. It was too weak to do the job I was pleading with it to do. I could make out fairly well running straight, but cutting and twisting to rush the passer was next to impossible.

There were several times that I could have put pressure on the passer, Don Meredith, if my ankle had been well. If I had been able to get to Meredith it might have been enough to change the whole complexion of the game. You can imagine how the frustration mounted when I couldn't do the job I wanted to do. Midway in the first quarter the Novocaine began to wear off a little, and by the middle of the second quarter it was really killing me.

I lost my temper

As we progressed through the second half, it was obvious that we were losing the game. Groaning inwardly, I thought, "It would sure help if I could do my job." The Cowboys had the ball and we were on the hash mark on the right side of the field. The play went to my left. Don Perkins was carrying, and he was breaking for the sideline. I had to get my hands on him.

Straining to the limit, I called on my sore and aching ankle to deliver, and it responded fairly well. I was about to make the tackle that would have taken Perkins out of bounds when Boeke plastered me. It was Glass and not Perkins who toppled out of bounds, and they picked up another eight yards on the play.

Boeke's block hurt my ankle, but it hurt my pride even more. In the heat of the moment I thought it was illegal, but later when the play was run on film, I knew it wasn't. I yelled at Boeke, "Cheap shot!" We were both mad.

Boeke hollered back, "Bill Glass, if you ask me, you're not even a Christian." Jim had read my first book entitled *Get In The Game* in which I had discussed the Christian perspective of pro

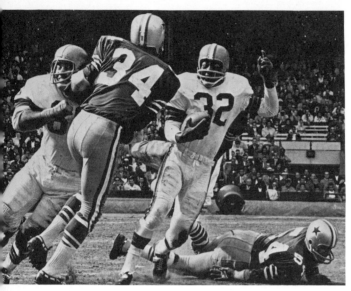

Jim Brown (32) in action against the Dallas Cowboys.

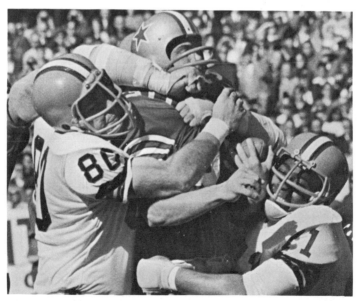

Walter Johnson (71) and Bill Glass (80) put the muscle on Dan Reeves (30), fullback, Dallas Cowboys.

football, so he knew where I stood. This hot-tempered exchange indicated two things: Jim had missed the point of my book, and I had let pain and frustration get the best of me.

Jim Boeke is a fine person

When we got back to Cleveland a letter from Boeke was waiting for me:

> Dear Bill:
> Guess you might call this a note of apology. I'm not apologizing for anything I did on the field, but for what I said on the field.
> I really had no right to say you were not a Christian on the field. I guess it all came out in the heat of the game. The block I threw on you was a good legal block and not a cheap out-of-bounds shot or one taken after the whistle had blown. When you said it was a chicken thing to do, it just reminded me of how Meredith must have felt when you blasted him in the mouth *after* he had thrown the ball last game. Certainly unnecessary shots like this after a quarterback has thrown the ball don't exemplify the qualities of a Christian athlete.
> For you and me yesterday's game seemed to be the battle of the cripples. Guess we were both hampered by our gimpy limbs. Even so, Bill, you are still the best end I have ever come up against. I hope your ankle heals soon.
> Sincerely,
> Jim Boeke

This letter was really welcome; it certainly humbled me. I couldn't remember hitting Meredith late, but I know the kind of pride offensive linemen have when it comes to protecting their quarterback. (The Kansas City linemen call their quarterback, Len Dawson, "Ajax" because they aim to keep him clean.) Undoubtedly I had, in the past, hit Meredith too often and too hard to please Boeke, but believe me, it wasn't enough to please me or my coaches. In eleven years of pro ball I've been penalized twice for hitting a quarterback late. Still, I never feel good about an illegal shot, regardless of whether the officials call it or not.

Nevertheless, I was overwhelmed by Boeke's letter. It was the first time I had received a letter from an opposing tackle, and I answered him immediately:

> Dear Jim:
>
> I'm sure you are a whole lot closer to right in this matter than I am. Your block was a close one. My problem was with a bad ankle and not with you. It was childish on my part!
>
> I don't remember hitting Don late, but probably I did. In the heat of the battle we always say and do a lot of things that we don't mean.
>
> Your statements about my not being a Christian weren't all that bad either. Lucky for me, sonship with God isn't affected by goodness or badness, but by relationship to Christ. Hope you win the championship since we can't.
>
> Sincerely,
Bill Glass

Can a pro football player be a Christian?

People frequently ask me in all earnestness how a pro football player can possibly be a Christian. They are unable to picture a Christian plowing into an opponent and slamming him to the ground. But this is just part of a game based on bodily contact. We never want to hurt the other guy. We just want to win and that demands rough, tough play.

I can say with complete honesty that in my eleven years of professional football, I have yet to face a tackle who I thought was trying to injure me. Sure, they all try to block me and knock me silly if they can, but I don't believe any player is actually trying to injure his opponent.

Professional football players are tough competitors, but we have a great respect for each other. We all know that the name of the game is *HIT*. But it's *HIT* hard to win, not *HIT* hard to hurt.

3

Football Drive Can Be Helpful in All of Life

Most of the players in professional football are involved in other professional or business interests. Early retirement is a fact of life—a man plays an average of four years. Of course, there are some who stick around for ten, fifteen, or twenty years, but most of us try to develop other business interests. During the off-season you will find players selling insurance, involved in real estate interests, dealing in cattle, playing the stock market, etc.

For example, Buddy Dial of the Dallas Cowboys is an excellent businessman with many and varied interests. Jim Houston and Lou Groza sell more life insurance in the off-season than most men would sell during an entire working year. Frank Ryan plans to teach at Rice University when he retires from football. He holds a Ph.D. in mathematics and teaches in the off-season now.

Players are usually aggressive businessmen

As a general rule, pro football players are highly successful businessmen because they have learned to carry the fight to the opposition. A professional in any field must be intensely aggressive. I've heard several business executives say that they prefer hiring athletes. One president of a large company commented, "I'd rather hire athletes because 1) they practice self-discipline; 2) they follow instructions; 3) they understand that there must be a head coach or boss that calls the shots; and 4) they fight harder, even after a bad call."

Contrary to the image held by some people, pro football players aren't big dumb brutes who know nothing about what's going on in the rest of the world. The majority are considerate, well-educated, patriotic, friendly family men who would succeed in a number of fields.

Caricatures aren't dependable

There are still those, however, who fail to see any possible connection between Christianity and pro football players—they fail to understand either the game or the way of life. They cling to outmoded caricatures of both football players and Christianity. On the one hand, the image of the big dumb brute of a player is just as unrealistic and untrue as the idea held by many people who visualize a Christian as an uninvolved, uninformed, näive dud. True, some Christians are extremely traditional, narrow-minded, and narrow-living, but to me, a part of Christian dedication is to penetrate every area of life.

Christianity has penetrated the field of professional football through the efforts of dedicated Christian players. Furthermore, Christianity has infiltrated a wide variety of places and situations because of pro football players who spend countless hours and untold energy in demonstrating this better way of life to young people around the country.

Christianity in pro football

Raymond Berry, formerly offensive end with the Baltimore Colts and now a coach with the Dallas Cowboys, is a close friend of mine and a dedicated Christian. He holds the lifetime pass receiving record in professional football. Raymond spends most of his off-season time in traveling over the country speaking to many groups about his relationship to Christ. He is closely associated with the Fellowship of Christian Athletes.

There are many other active F.C.A. members in football. In 1967 Tom Landry, head coach of the Dallas Cowboys, asked me to be a speaker at an F.C.A. retreat he was organizing for the Dallas area. There were over one hundred high school and college coaches in the Dallas area who attended out of respect for Landry and his Christian faith. In addition, there are players like Fran Tarkenton, Maxie Baughn, and Don Shinnick who are very articulate and bold in expressing their faith.

Over fifty star athletes have contributed to F.C.A. books, *The Courage to Conquer* and *The Goal and the Glory*. Frank Broyles and Paul Dietzel are just two of the many college coaches associated with F. C. A.

The Fellowship of Christian Athletes—a great influence

A young boy who recently attended an F.C.A. retreat said: "At first I didn't want to go. But when they said that Bill Curry, Don Shinnick, Raymond Berry, Jerry Stovall, and Paul Anderson were going to be there, I said I'd go. So I did. I went to see my gods, and I heard my gods talk about their God. Before the week was over, their God became my God."

Many outstanding athletes are beginning to realize the importance of their influence on young people and all sports fans. The youth of our country are engaged in a fervent search for a cause —for a sense of meaning and involvement. This is my greatest challenge—I want to do my part in showing them the *greatest cause*.

Prayer in pro football

For over twenty years our Cleveland team has stopped for prayer before every game. These last moments in the dressing room are heavy with excitement and nervous tension. I'm sure that every player must feel a lot like I do—desperate and scared. Outside, the huge crowd roars with noisy expectancy. The probing eye of the television camera will expose our every move. The pressure to win is great, and even though I've been a pro for twelve years, I still get nervous.

At the last moment the coaches, trainers, and equipment men leave the dressing room, and we are alone. You get the feeling they're saying by leaving, "We've done all we can; now it's all up to you." The room is quiet. Our captain speaks in excited tones for two or three minutes, and then asks, "Does anyone else have anything to say before our prayer?" Usually, one or two players make some comment. For a number of years one of the veterans used to say, "Yea, let me have a word." And then he'd launch into a flight of oratory, sprinkling every sentence with profanity. He seemed to take special delight in hurling all kinds of incriminating insults at the ancestry of our opponents for the day. After concluding this highly descriptive and sulfuric tirade, he would kneel in prayer with his teammates. He always exercised the same fervency in repeating the Lord's Prayer, but his choice of language and tone of voice was a bit more reverent.

The new breed in pro football

Admittedly, a lot of players couldn't be referred to as saints. But, unfortunately, all too few people know about Raymond Berry, Don Shinnick, Fran Tarkenton, Prentice Gautt, Jerry Stovall, Roman Gabriel, Monte Clark, and that whole new breed of athletes that are a part of F.C.A. In fact, there are few players, if any, who don't have some sort of faith in God. It is quite surprising at times to see some of the outwardly indifferent men remain on their knees in silent prayer after the Lord's Prayer has been repeated in unison by the entire team.

Every team in the league has some sort of chapel service on Sunday morning for the Protestant members of the team, while the Catholic players usually go out to mass. Frequently, we invite a minister or an articulate layman to speak at our service—usually held in a room at the hotel. As a rule, our service consists of an opening prayer, a devotional message, discussion, and a closing prayer. When visiting teams come to Cleveland, they often ask me to get speakers for them.

On one occasion, we were scheduled to play Washington, and they asked me to get a speaker for their chapel service. Twenty-five of their players and Otto Graham, their head coach, were there. Otto arrived just in time to hear Paul Krause, defensive back for the Redskins, introduce the speaker. Paul said, "I'd like to introduce Garry Kinder, a friend of Bill Glass." Garry said later, "I was looking right at Otto as he came into the room. When he heard Krause say, 'a friend of Bill Glass,' Otto did a real double take." Injecting the name of an "enemy" into the introduction just four hours before game time certainly didn't contribute toward a relaxed situation. But Garry evidently handled it all right, because Otto said that he was the best speaker they had ever had. Bobby Mitchell, who was seated on the front row, commented to me after the game, "That chapel speaker was the greatest."

Monte Clark, our offensive right tackle, told me that the most inspiring speech he ever heard was made by Tom Landry, head coach of the Dallas Cowboys. At the time Monte was with the Cowboys. It was Landry's first speech of the year to the team, and he opened by saying, "Men, we're going to get along if you don't cross me in any one of three areas. The most important thing in the world to me is my commitment to Christ. The second area of importance is my family, and the third is this ball club. I want what's best for all three, and if you don't, we may not get along." Landry is one of the few coaches who personally leads his team in prayer before every game.

The Christian faith brings comradeship
A few years ago a Methodist minister in Cleveland telephoned me and said, "I just got a call from Charlie Johnson of the St. Louis Cardinals [we were going to play them that week]. He

asked me to conduct a service for their Protestant players at 9:00 A.M. Sunday morning, the day they play you guys." The minister went on to ask if I thought it would be appropriate for me to participate in the service. I declined because of the possible danger of being misunderstood. Meeting with them wouldn't have affected either my play on the field or theirs, but if an unsympathetic sportswriter had gotten wind of it and played it up in some twisted way, it could have looked bad. Maybe I should have gone ahead; it was tempting because I enjoy doing this kind of thing. At any rate, I was reminded again of the widespread interest in Christianity in professional football.

Prior to one of our games in Cleveland with the Dallas Cowboys, Buddy Dial, one of their pass receivers, called and asked me to get a speaker for their Sunday morning devotional meeting.

Soon after I checked into my hotel room on Saturday, the telephone rang—it was Buddy. He wanted to know if I had arranged for the speaker. I assured him it was all taken care of and that Sam Bender would be there. "Great," he said. "Sam really wowed them last year when he spoke for us."

While we were talking, I could hear a voice in the background —it was Don Meredith, the Cowboy quarterback. Buddy excused himself for a minute and then came back on the line: "Bill, Don says to tell you to remember that you are a Christian when you're rushing him tomorrow." We both laughed. But after I hung up I thought: *If I remember my Christian commitment, I'll just bust him harder.*

4

Emotions That Produce Peak Performance

Football is a game that must be played emotionally. In an intense, exhausting sport a player must have strong emotional motivation to put out what it takes. There are a number of reasons which can provide the player with the almost irrational persistence needed to keep going in this rough game.

Fans and popularity furnish strong motivation for some

Some players gloat over their popularity—they really work hard for the fans' approval. This is a pretty good motivation for the high school or college player whose whole world revolves around popularity and the adoration of the girls. In professional football, popularity with the fans isn't the prime motivation, but now and then it does give you a lift. I got a letter a year or so ago from a boy in New York who wrote: "I have followed your career in pro football closely. I think you are the greatest football player in the country. I watch every move you make when I see you on TV. I would like to start a fan club for you. Could you send me an autographed picture of yourself?"

This really makes you feel good. It's worth almost any effort to improve yourself just to have fans like that, and it certainly made me want to work harder on my goals. A little later I noticed another player had gotten a letter similar to mine, and as I looked further, almost every player on our team had one—it was mimeographed. It's a funny thing though; I've noticed that the fan mail is much heavier when we are winning.

Fans are fickle

Fair weather friends hang around the dressing room or meet us at the airport after we win. After we win a key game, the crowd that meets us at the airport is huge, sometimes as many as ten thousand. But when we lose, there may not be over a hundred people. The only people you can always count on to be there at the airport after an "away" game are our wives.

I remember one year we came in late at night after getting beat. As our plane touched down at Hopkins Airport, someone said jokingly, "I bet the crowd will be huge to welcome us back this week." The week before we had won and a large crowd had greeted us. But this week we had lost. Someone else said, "Yeah, they'll be out by the thousands, brass band and all to welcome home the conquering heroes."

As we taxied down the runway and up toward the terminal, I looked through my window into the snowy night. I saw no one out on the observation deck—the week before it had been jammed by thousands of yelling fans. I saw no TV camera crews outside our gate with their equipment set up for interviews and pictures of the team returning—they'd been there with bells on the week before. Last week fans had crowded the airport so that you had to push your way through the crowds for a hundred yards and even out to your car in the parking lot.

Someone on the team, reacting to the same things I was, yelled, "Man, how they love a winner." But, when we came down the steps and walked up to the gate, there were our wives holding a huge sign which read, "We love you Browns."

I thought, "Yes, you are the only ones. But then, what more could a man want?"

Football fans are funny. The kids really idolize you, and I wouldn't minimize the impact a ball player can have for good. Big-name players, and even lesser stars, have had a tremendous influence on young fans. We can sell everything from Christianity to cigarettes and beer by endorsements.

On the other hand, football fans are fickle. They yell themselves hoarse for you, and when you make a big play, they really remember it—sometimes for an entire day. But more than anything else, the interest the fans have in you is conditioned on whether or not you win (some just so they can collect their bets). Others have a great loyalty to the Browns and have been coming to games ever since they can remember. They have season tickets and would come, win, lose, or draw. I am continually amazed by how much they know about what's going on with the team. These are the real fans.

Naturally, they want to see you win, but they are still loyal when you lose.

Popularity as a player is short-lived

There's no doubt about it: athletic popularity is short-lived and shouldn't be depended upon. There was a big-name ball player who retired after some of his fair-weather fans had promised him big important jobs. He sat at home for a year waiting for a job to come through, but it never did. Finally, he went out and got a job on his own and is now doing great. It took him a year to wake up to the fact that he had depended too much on football success. My point is that self-improvement either in pro football or anywhere else has to come from some deeper motive than the response of the fans.

As far as I'm concerned, the fans I work for the hardest are my own two sons. In 1966 while playing against Washington, I came out with my first injury in over twenty years of football.

My little son Bobby slipped past the policeman at the dressing room door and came up to the training table where I was stretched out groaning over my badly twisted ankle. With trainers, coaches, and players crowded around, Bobby said, "Daddy, I think you are the best football player in the whole world." What more could a father want?

The motive for self-improvement is a complex thing

One of the goals set by the coaching staff of any pro football team is self-improvement. They continually harp on the value of the individual player and on the teamwork principle. The entire concept of practice and scrimmage is to give the player opportunity to improve himself both as an individual and as a member of the team.

Every man has a private complex of reasons as to why he either does or does not seek to improve himself. We all know that the practice sessions alone will not bring about the desired result. It is a part of the psychology of the successful team that the coaches are able to find the key to the motives that will set each player on fire for self-improvement. For many players, this key to success is never found, either by the coaching staff or by the player himself. He goes about his task working at about one-half efficiency, if that much.

Every player, just like every Christian or every politician or any person who devotes his life to a cause, should constantly seek things that "turn him on" and propel him toward maximum productivity. This kind of self-analysis doesn't come easily. The chances are that once you have found the combination to "turning your energies on" full force, you will have discovered that the combination works no matter what your task. I have found that the disciplines that make me a better Christian are the same as those that help me do my best on the football field. In fact, I don't divide these areas of my life at all. To the Christian, every activity is sacred.

Money is not a powerful enough motive

I am sure that many players play the game for the money. You can be almost certain that a high-bonus rookie who has dollar signs in front of his eyes won't be able to see the football for the dollar signs. He just won't put out what it takes for maximum effectiveness. If I played football just for the money, I would have quit long ago. Not that the hope of a better contract, or the promise of a raise after a good year doesn't motivate you; it just doesn't motivate you enough for the *supreme* effort.

Some players work hard for the team and the coaches

Liking or fearing the coaches will often inspire you to really put out. But to know that your teammates are depending on you is an even greater motivation. Personal pride makes you want to hold your corner and fulfill your assignment whatever it is, because you just wouldn't be able to face your teammates and the coaches after making a mess of things.

Probably, the main reason most of us are anxious for the approval and respect of our fellow players and coaches is that they are the only ones who really know just how well a man does. The average fan or sportswriter doesn't know enough about the game to judge accurately a player's performance. First, they don't know what your assignment is on a given play. Second, they don't see many of the important maneuvers because their attention is fixed on the ball carrier or passer. For example, as a defensive end, there's nothing I do that the normal fan notices except making a great tackle or hitting the quarterback before he releases the pass. There are many other important factors involved in my play that only the coaches or a teammate would be able to understand and appreciate. The fans may think you played a great game when you really made many mistakes.

Players are always eager to give one another credit for achievements. I know how much it means to the other players to get a little pat on the back, because it means so much to me. Some coaches have the capacity to bring out almost fanatical zeal in players. But again, this is more of a factor in college than it is in pro football.

In professional ball the coaches are respected and admired, but there are few Bear Bryants. It isn't that the college coaches are better psychologists than our coaches, but the drives and motivations of the players are different.

To continue to improve, a player must have an inner drive that demands that last ounce of effort so necessary to achievement—you have to want it desperately. It isn't enough to please your wife, your coach, or even your adoring little son who honestly thinks you are the greatest. You can fool all of these people, but you can't fool yourself. You'll know whether or not you could have hit a little harder, pursued a little more relentlessly, etc.

Some humanist philosophers think that man is the only God there is, that men are little gods themselves. Obviously, I don't agree with that. There is a definite sense in which God dwells inside you, and being true to yourself is a deep recognition of the God who made you what you are and what you can become. Look at it this way: a Christian cannot be satisfied with himself unless he pleases God.

Most Negro players are trying to prove something. I'm sure that if I were a Negro I'd be motivated to a super performance as a means of furthering the cause of racial justice. In my opinion, this is one reason Jim Brown was so great. He was trying to prove himself to the world and fight for the Negro cause. This was a factor in his retirement; he felt that younger Negro players like Gale Sayers and Leroy Kelly could take up where he left off. He also felt that a movie and acting career would extend his own influence in behalf of civil rights.

Actually, the pro game is so demanding that if a player doesn't have some gut issue motivating him, he won't do as well. I think this is one of the reasons that there are a number of dedicated Christians who have done well in the game. As Christians, we feel compelled to be more than mediocre for Christ's sake.

Jim Brown (32) in action against New York.

Bill Glass and Jim Brown.

Humility is a fine thing in many ways

How do you define humility? The Bible speaks of this quality as a virtue. But what is it? The dictionary defines humility as "freedom from arrogance." That helps us some, but we need to take a closer look. I know a good many sincere people who define humility this way: "Good guys always finish last, and they smile and accept it."

That is certainly an unacceptable definition to me. I don't believe a person is expected to hold back one iota so someone else can get ahead. As a matter of fact, I think a person is letting everybody down, including himself and God, if he doesn't put out his last gasp of energy in order to be first. I don't think that humility means that "good guys" always finish either first or last; neither do I feel that humility means that any of us should be mediocre.

Remember too, it isn't necessary to be mediocre just so you won't hurt the feelings of your mediocre friends. For example, if I play my game at half speed and you come out on top, you can be just as humble as I am. Your attitude will not be one of arrogance, but it will be one of healthy pride, and a feeling that you have lived up to God's plan for your life. He gave each of us this potential, and you must use it to the maximum. You should never trade your feeling of having reached the peak of what God equipped you to do for a feeling of humility based on mediocre performance.

Make your comparisons with the best

It is an escapable fact, as every talent scout knows, that a player's ability can never be judged properly unless he is in competition of the highest quality. Every now and then a rookie is brought in from some small conference back in the hill country. He has completed more passes and has made more touchdown passes than anyone in history. So, the scouts go out and watch him in his final game; he looks phenomenal and is signed to a pro contract. There are some notable exceptions, but many of them wash out during training camp. Their abilities had not been tested in stiff competition. If a college player was tops in one of the strong conferences, we know more of what to expect. But even this isn't always dependable. I have found that comparing myself to the best rather than to second-best is a real asset to my own efforts at self-improvement. If I were the best pass rusher on our team, I couldn't rest on my laurels. I'd have to try to be the best in the league. It's the other teams in the league that are our competition. I must try to be as effective rushing that passer as Deacon Jones and Willie Davis, and I'd better never forget it, because my self-improvement depends on it.

At the same time, I know that I have some definite weaknesses. I'm not as fast as I'd like to be, and, although I can do better by working at it, it is a definite limitation. Nevertheless, I must struggle to improve this and other weaknesses.

In playing any game, don't be afraid to compare yourself with the best. Take proper pride in your accomplishments, but don't become self-satisfied. Self-satisfaction is deadly in pro football; it is just as deadly in the games some of you may be playing. It's like Paul says: "I press toward the prize of the high calling of God in Christ Jesus." Paul knew that he was a worthy disciple of Christ, but he held up the best as his example. Christ should be an example for all of us.

Part 2
The Challenge
of the Unexpected

5

From Club to Club

After graduating from college, my new bride and I climbed into our 1957 station wagon and drove to Canada for my first season of pro football. This was a happy time for us, and we had some enjoyable times during our season in the north country. But, Mavis and I were both South Texans, and the sub-zero Saskatchewan winter had us fighting colds and flu most of the time.

Canadian football is entirely different from the American game. It was difficult for me to adjust to a twelve man team, no downfield blocking after ten yards, no time outs, a longer and wider field, and a number of other rule differences. After winding up our first season, we decided not to return for a second year, In addition to the weather and the differences in Canadian football, I felt our decision had providential overtones.

Back in the United States

During our stay in Canada, we were completely cut off from contacts and influences in the United States. This caused us a great deal of concern, because I felt that my main reason for being in football was to take advantage of the many opportunities it offered to witness for Christ (this isn't to imply that Canada is unimportant). I couldn't escape from the growing feeling that God was leading us back to the States. Humanly speaking, it would have been much easier to stay in Canada. My Canadian team management had agreed to release me after the first season if I wanted to return to the States. But, this was an oral agreement, and my written contract contained the usual option clause. Then too, I had no assurance of making a ball club if we went back to the States. However, when the 1958 season rolled around, I was given the opportunity to play for the Detroit Lions. Saskatchewan honored their verbal agreement, but I was one of the few players released from a Canadian team without a court fight. Possibly, they figured that I wasn't much of a loss after my dismal showing the previous season.

Detroit had won the NFL championship during my year in Canada. They were overconfident and anxious to point out my mistake in going to Canada in the first place. I was trying to break into a club that was loaded with veterans, and they weren't giving up without a fight. We started out the year by getting clobbered by the All-Stars in Chicago. As the season progressed, we moved steadily from bad to worse. But, my wife and I were convinced that we had done the right thing in making our move. In the four years that followed, both my fortune and Detroit's were better. I won the starting assignment at defensive right end, and we went to the second-place bowl at Miami three times.

Being traded

I don't remember what night of the week it was, but Mavis and I had been out until about 10:30. We heard the phone ringing as we opened the door, and we rushed to answer it. It was Waddy Spoelstra, a sportswriter for *Detroit News* and a very close friend.

Waddy had become a Christian about six months before I had met him; he had been a tough, two-fisted reporter and lived the part up to the hilt. But, one day his teen-age daughter was stricken with a brain aneurysm and lay for days at the point of death. Waddy got on his knees in the hospital chapel and promised God that if He would spare the girl, he would sur-

render all that was left of his life to Christ. The girl was spared, and Waddy had a genuine conversion experience. I was privileged to know him during the early stages of his growth as a Christian.

At any rate, Waddy called to tell me that George Wilson had been trying to reach me all day. "I've got some bad news for you, Bill," he said. "You've been traded to Cleveland. George will be calling you in a little while, and I wanted you to be pre-

Watson Spoelstra
Detroit News

pared." I had had four wonderful years at Detroit. Waddy had been one of my prime sources of encouragement during my stay there: He was in tears when he called and so were Mavis and I. Waddy's friendship was probably one of our greatest experiences during the Detroit years, although we had had many wonderful associations.

I was prepared when George called. He was nervous and seemed to have difficulty telling me about the trade. He started off like Waddy did: "Bill, I have some bad news. We've traded you to Cleveland. We didn't want to, but they wouldn't agree to a trade unless they got you. I wanted Milt Plum, and they wanted Jim Ninoski."

Being traded brings out confused emotions

Being traded is a blow to the ego, and it is confusing. It does mean that a team wants you, but it also means that your present team considers you expendable. This is difficult for a player to take in stride. After all, there is a lot involved in switching teams.

Jim Garcia was traded to the New York Giants about midway through the 1966 training camp. Coach Collier explained that Jim would probably have a better chance of playing more with New York than he had with us. This was probably true because Garcia had been the backup man for Paul Wiggin and me at defensive end during 1965, and he had seen very little action. However, regardless of the explanations, we all feel sick when we get the news; I know that I felt sick when Detroit traded me.

Ball club management has a wide variety of reasons for trading. The issue in Garcia's case was created when Jim Brown quit the team. The coaches had to go out and trade for new running backs. At this particular time, the Browns needed backs more than linemen. Neither Wig nor I had been hurt much in the past, and they could always move a tackle over to fill in if we were injured.

As usual, a lot of the guys congregated in Garcia's room to wish him luck and encouragement. When Mo (Dick Modzelewski) came in, someone said, "Mo, give him the scoop on New York." Modzelewski had been with the Giants for ten years before coming to Cleveland.

"Tell the guys hello for me. You're going to a good outfit."

What else is there to say? At a time like this a man needs friends, but, more than anything else, he needs to get off by himself and think things through. After a time, it doesn't hurt so much.

I've thought about retiring

To be perfectly honest, I had strong thoughts of retiring when I got hurt during the latter part of the 1966 season. If a player retires after suffering an injury, people won't think that he chickened out. Furthermore, his own self-image remains intact.

Over the years most of us are tempted to retire several times. Then a man has a good season, and he goes back for just one more year. The "one more years" stretch out until—well, who knows how long? Lou Groza is still going strong after more than twenty years. I'm sure that Lou thought about retiring after being the goat in the second Dallas game of 1966. But he finished up the year strong and was back for 1967 The retirements that affected me the most were those of my two best friends, Jim Shofner and Paul Wiggin. Shof retired and went into coaching in 1964; Wig followed suit in 1968. They are both coaching with San Francisco.

A professional football player has his ups and downs. We are tempted to retire, and then we get to thinking—the next year may be our biggest. So far, it has been right for me to stay in the game. My football has been a great platform from which to communicate my faith.

6

Injury

Every football player is haunted by fear of injury. This apprehension is based not on fear of pain or discomfort but on the knowledge that injury results in inability to help the team—it can change a star into a "has been" without any warning.

The possibility of injury can't be ignored

We are vulnerable to injury in any one of a dozen critical places, but knee damage is the most serious. A player can stay in the game with a bad hand or arm, but never with an injured knee. As a rule, a bad knee injury demands surgery—the results of which determine the player's future.

A number of things can jeopardize a man's career: injury, illness, trades. But the most humiliating is to be benched in favor of a younger player the coaches think is more capable. We always know that sooner or later we're going to be out of there, but we dread the day.

Every player wants to be in the game. Sitting on the bench for any reason is pure torture to the guy with a burning desire to play. But injury is the deadliest of the knockout blows because we never know when it may happen. Rookies are particularly apprehensive about being hurt, because, in a way, they have more at stake. However, every player lives in fear of the crippling blow that could end his career.

You never know how it really feels until you've been there

Frank Parker, a big old country boy who used to play for us, gave me insight into the feelings of an injured player, although it didn't really sink in fully until after my own injury in 1966. Frank had a bad knee injury a few years ago, so bad that he had to lay out a full season. He had major surgery and was unable to play during 1965.

When Frank came back to the club for the 1966 season, he was the epitome of gratefulness. He'd say, "I'm just so glad to be back here with you guys that I don't know what to do. It's really tough to have to work for a living down in the poor country of Oklahoma." This last part was said as a joke, because the idea of hard work on the outside isn't what concerns us. What Frank was trying to say was that an injured player is a displaced and frustrated person unless he is with the team and in the game. When a man is robbed of his chance to play for any reason, he is denied the right of being himself—it's a first cousin to dying.

My only injury came against Washington in 1966

I played twenty years of football without an injury—ten as an amateur and ten in the pros—but I never considered myself to be a superman who couldn't get hurt.

And then it happened. We were ahead of Washington by thirteen points with one minute left in the game. One of their guards clipped me with what I felt was "a real cheap shot." My ankle was hurt, and I was pretty sure that I had a bad sprain. Leo Murphy, our trainer, wrapped the ankle tightly to keep down the swelling. Several teammates and sportswriters asked how I felt, and I assured them and the coaches that I was all right. I even jogged a little to prove to them and myself that I could do it. After the game, Mavis and I went out to eat with friends. There I sat, with ice bags wrapped around my ankle, reassuring everybody that it was really nothing and that I'd be ready to play in the next game.

I was injured just four days before we were to meet Dallas on Thanksgiving Day. This was to be a decisive game; the winner would take the divisional championship. The tension began to build up in me. We didn't have any replacements for defensive ends. With Jim Brown's decision to quit the team at the beginning of the season, most of the trading and recruiting had been built around running backs. Paul Wiggin and I were carrying the whole load at defensive end. We did have four defensive tackles, and one of them could switch over to defensive end, but without having played the position, the odds were poor that he could do well.

But I was only kidding myself

When I got up the next morning, I could hardly walk. I was in for trouble. With a full week to pamper my ankle, I could possibly be ready, but with only four days, it just didn't seem possible. Dr. Ippilitto, the team physician, shot it with cortisone later in the day, and it did seem to improve. But I didn't work out with the rest of the team that day or the next. I did manage to hop through workout on Wednesday before we left for Dallas. With the use of ice, cortisone, and ultrasound, we attempted to get an injury ready in four days that should have taken two to three weeks to heal.

Before the game they shot my ankle with Novocaine, and for the first fifteen minutes it was like playing on a stump— I couldn't feel a thing. During the next thirty minutes, my leg began to throb with pain, and I couldn't get the push off the ankle that I needed to rush the passer. We fought a desperate battle, but Dallas beat us and captured the divisional championship. I like to play every down of every game, so I was determined to play in spite of the injury.

I never fully recovered from my injury during the 1966 season

I was a cripple for the rest of the season, but I did have a stroke of luck in the game against New York. We were playing on a frozen field, and somehow that seemed to work in my favor We wore tennis shoes because the field was frozen too hard for cleats. My ankle held up beautifully, and although we were behind thirty-one to fourteen at the half, we went on to win. My big thrill came when I picked up a loose ball after Walter Johnson had clobbered their quarterback, and ran sixteen yards for the only touchdown of my pro career. Accidents will happen!

That comeback win and accidental touchdown were sweet. Not sweet enough, however, to cushion the blow of not winning the championship and thereby losing the opportunity of playing in the first Super Bowl game.

Part 3
The Challenge
of Discipline

7

Pride in Pro Football

"Pride goes before the fall." These familiar and often quoted words of Scripture seem to refer essentially to a destructive, arrogant pride that infiltrates to the very core of life, producing a disdainful and superior attitude toward events and people. But there is a form of pride that is absolutely essential for a football player, as it is for anyone. It develops out of a quiet self-confidence and assurance, and it evolves into a dynamic life concept characterized by achievement and self-acceptance.

There is a fine distinction here that is seldom considered or emphasized. Arrogance and feelings of superiority are despicable and destructive attitudes which the Bible refers to as sin, and this is true. But the kind of pride that inspires the will to win, the ambition to succeed by utilizing to the full one's God-given abilities is another thing. I believe this quality is an essential factor in football and in all of life.

I bet on myself in football

If I am to improve and excel, I must bet on myself. If I don't think big, I'll wind up flat on my back with the ball carrier slamming right through the hole where I was supposed to be, and making the first down before the linebacker can come up for the tackle.

I find that confidence in my own ability to hold my corner or to get to the passer spells the difference. This is not to say that I can do *anything* merely because I think I can. But if I didn't believe in my ability to achieve my goals, I wouldn't accomplish a thing. A low opinion of ourselves is not a virtue either on or off the field of play. The difference is that on the field we need a quiet self-confidence that almost approaches arrogance, while off the field, we need a calm self-assurance that implies belief in ourselves and in others. People won't resent our feelings of confidence as long as our attitude helps them to believe in themselves.

The football player lives in a world of self-images

Possibly a football player is not much different from anyone else, but I do believe he lives a bit more in a world of self-images. However, there are some self-images that are especially detrimental. This is why so many rookies fall by the wayside—they don't hold the right images.

To begin with, a player cannot have a second-string picture of himself. He must be a first-stringer in his mind before he can make the first team. For nearly eleven years of pro football, I've been playing in every game. True, I've been fortunate in not being injured, but I don't credit it all to that. The fact is, I never even entertain the possibility of anyone moving me out, or of getting hurt. The objective of every effective player is to do a good job. He must think of the ways in which he is going to succeed and not of the possibilities of failure.

God gets the credit

I would be afraid not to say that prime credit for everything goes to God. But it is not really fear that makes me say this; it's gratitude for His help and guidance. I'm totally undeserving of anything. Yet, He has given me a healthy body capable of doing the job, and He has called me into this unusual vocation.

I feel that I'm the most fortunate person alive. All of my interests and activities are enjoyable, and I have the most compatible, dedicated, and beautiful Christian family in the world. Sure, I'm prejudiced. Prime human credit goes to my wonderful wife; she furnishes all of the beauty for the family.

Even the hard things in life seem easy with God's help. It is difficult to drag my family back and forth between our six-month-homes in Waco, Texas, and Cleveland, Ohio. Getting in top physical shape every year is more of a struggle as I get older. Our children have to adjust to new schools and friends twice a year. And Mavis and I fight a constant battle to be accepted both by those athletes who don't always understand our Christian stance and by those Christians who don't always understand our athletic way of life. But, our problems and concerns are negligible in comparison to those of Christians in other parts of the world who are really called on to suffer deeply for Christ's sake.

Some players have a victim-image

Many rookies fail to make it because they live with a victim-image—they believe the world is against them. They think the coach or the players have it in for them. Every adverse thing that happens is blamed on someone or something supposedly beyond their control. They rationalize: "I'm a receiver and this club doesn't need any receivers." Or they use any one of a thousand different excuses, from injury to not having a chance to show what they can do, to cover up for their fear and lack of confidence. None of this means a thing if a player has what it takes.

I believe that God cares deeply for His children and that His guidance in life is unmistakable within the context of His will. Beyond that, I think a person makes or breaks himself. A person's worst enemy is often himself, especially if he carries the victim-image. In saying this, I don't mean that we should cut God out. It just seems that our tendency is to inhibit His use of us.

Try trusting God in the world in which you live. Make up

your mind that the things which happen are the result of what
you are doing about this game of life. You'll get the breaks if you
make them.

Frequently, we all hear people say apologetically, "I'm only
human." True enough, but why use this as an excuse for being
less of a human than you could be?

8

Positive Picturing Really Works

In a 1965 game against the New York Giants, Jim Brown gained almost 200 yards rushing. Some running backs would be glad to gain this much in an entire season. He literally ran wild that day. I had been playing with Jim for a number of years and had watched him closely, but there was something different about Jim on this particular day. He was always great, but this time he was even greater than usual.

Jim Brown used the power of imagination
I could hardly wait to get Jim aside and talk with him. "How in the world did you do it, Jim?" I asked.

"What do you mean?"

"How did you get so fired up for the game psychologically?"

"You wouldn't believe it if I told you."

"Just try me."

"Well, I'll tell you, Bill, I've been playing this game all during the past week. Everywhere I've gone I've been playing this game. As I sat in my room, as I drove my car, as I lay in bed, I have been imagining this game—playing it over and over . . . I could just see myself taking the ball from Frank, breaking tackles, sweeping the ends, sliding through and over tackles, and eluding the linebackers. I saw myself catching passes—running over, around, and through people. So, when the game finally arrived, it wasn't new to me. I felt I had already been there, and I just did what I had been seeing myself do all week. It was so real in my imagination that it was like a stage play."

It works for me

I can tell you now that this method is nothing short of phenomenal. At least it works for me. This is much stronger than positive thinking; it is *positive picturing*. I first became interested in this two years before Jim told me that he practiced it. A friend of mine in the selling field encouraged me to read a book entitled *Psycho-Cybernetics* by Dr. Maxwell Maltz. I found it very interesting and started practicing some of the pyschological disciplines that the book suggests. I don't think Jim ever read the book; it was just a natural thing with him. In fact, I believe that every great athlete and successful person in any field does, either consciously or unconsciously, what this book suggests—see yourself doing your job well in your imagination.

Writing it down clinches it in your mind

The techniques of positive picturing may well vary from person to person. Jim Brown had only to think about it. I find that it is much more effective for me to write down the things I want to visualize. In preparing for a game I write down everything that I might experience on a piece of paper—warming up, feeling relaxed but intense and ready, crossing the sideline onto the playing field. I sense the power and strength surging through me.

I visualize myself firing across the line into my opponent, playing the trap, block, the double-team, or rushing the passer, faking inside and cutting outside, getting to the passer. I write all of this down in words and sketch it on a piece of paper, and then

I close my eyes and see it happening. With positive picturing I try to get ready to face any situation that may arise. I do this every day for at least thirty minutes.

It seems to me that the best time for intensive positive picturing is an hour or so before the game. I try to get off to myself, take out my notes, and go over them for the last time. But, it would be entirely useless to do it just this one time. This concept must become a whole new way of thinking before it can be entirely effective.

Don't confuse prayer and positive picturing

Many people ask me if I pray before going onto the field. Yes, I do pray. I ask God to give me the capacity to be my best self. God should not be ruled out of any part of life, and I believe He will be with me if I ask Him. It is really up to me to allow Him to animate the abilities He has already given me. He understands my psychological make-up because He created it. And, it's imperative to be in tune with His created work physically and psychologically. Imagination (positive picturing) is required to bring out that potential, but I see this as a psychological process, not a spiritual one. This is just as much a psychological discipline as weight lifting is a physical discipline. God intends for me to develop myself in every area of life. And my football career is a spiritual activity in that it is a way of sharing my faith.

Some people make a habit of running themselves down

Unfortunately, many people use positive picturing in reverse. They visualize themselves making mistakes. You see, whatever a person sees himself doing in his imagination tends to come true.

Do you make it a practice of running yourself down? If so, you are actually making a negative suggestion, and you are pre-conditioning yourself to failure. Deprecation of self is a sickness that is frequently used to call attention to oneself.

Watch the pitfalls of mental picturing

To be effective, positive picturing must be based on good technique. For example, if I picture myself making a certain play, but I visualize its execution incorrectly from the point of view of basic fundamentals, I'll make mistakes through positive picturing.

The most important job of a defensive end is to rush the passer. So, I've had a tendency to concentrate on the pass rush and not on the running game. At one point I found myself rushing the passer on every play and failing to concentrate on the running game. Coach Collier pointed out my weakness repeatedly and said, "Bill, you should consider every play a running play and read the pass as it shows" (a pass play usually is apparent immediately because the tackle drops back for a pass protection block). In order to correct this weakness I started picturing myself playing more running plays, thus alerting my subconscious to the importance of the running play.

You should not expect immediate results from this discipline any more than you should expect immediate results from any form of practice. When I first tried it, I expected instant improvement, but was doomed to disappointment. It takes time, but it works.

Then too, I made the mistake of depending too heavily on this technique. I've played some poor games simply because of the notion that positive picturing was all that was necessary. But, I've discovered that a burning desire to achieve is essential as well.

Keep in mind that this is merely an extension of your practice on the field, with the added advantage of always doing well in imagination. The nervous system can't tell the difference between actual practice and vividly imagined practice.

Don't practice your mistakes

Blanton Collier says a thousand times a season, "Before you can improve, you must be willing to admit you're wrong." So, in reality I should be grateful when one of the coaches points out a basic mistake, but, like everyone else, I have my immature emotional reactions of resentment toward criticism. However, I can't afford to continue picturing myself doing something wrong, since a wrong mental picture will guide me to failure just as a right one will guide me to success.

Many people practice and practice, but they practice their mistakes. Golf is a perfect example. Suppose that you are a slicer —the more you practice, the more you slice. Why? Because you are driving the bad habit deeper into your nervous system every time you hit the ball.

You may be doing this same thing in your Christian life and social relationships—driving people farther and farther away from you. If you are a failure in your Christian life, ask God to give you the insight and then practice doing things the right way— both in your imagination and in actuality.

9

The Taste of Defeat - Bitter

During the time that Blanton Collier was head coach at the University of Kentucky, they went through a sustained losing streak. He often says, "I've tasted the bitter dregs of defeat, and I know how awful it is. You just don't know how to appreciate the sweetness of victory until you've scraped around the bottom among the bitter dregs as I have." I've never known a man who so detested the very thought of losing.

I play to win

Actually, I'm not a good loser, either. I don't intend to be, and I don't apologize for it. As a rule, *good losers usually lose.* It doesn't hurt them enough, so they don't give that last ounce of effort that makes the difference. The immortal Grantland Rice wrote: "When that great scorer comes to write against your name, it doesn't matter whether you've won or lost, but how you've played the game." I think I know what he meant, but there's still the possibility of using it as a crutch.

Undoubtedly, there's something to be said for taking a loss gracefully, but I'd rather not take a loss at all. Perhaps one of the most distorted notions perpetrated by man's rationalizations is that God is on the side of the loser. Eternal rewards are not based on merit points earned in the game. God's judgment is administered according to whether or not we play the game on *His* team. It is the choice of teams that is of first importance. If we aren't on His team, it is impossible to win. And if we are on His team, we just can't lose.

Throughout my career I've played on teams that have lost, but for the most part, I've played on winning teams, and I want to keep it that way. Of course, there is a sense in which winning or losing is a relative thing. The apostle Paul said, "I count everything as gain for Christ." He didn't lose because he refused to think in terms of losses or defeats. Paul's sole concern was in "keeping the faith." When he and Silas were thrown into jail, they were locked in chains. Outwardly, it appeared that they were lost, but they spent their time singing praises to God, and theirs was the ultimate victory.

There are no moral victories in pro football

I believe, however, that this analogy breaks down in pro football. There are no *moral* victories. After Green Bay clobbered us in the 1965 championship game, the coaches didn't say a word. We had been badly beaten. In complete disgust Mo said, "We all stunk out the joint." We were miserable failures that day, and we knew it.

In the 1966 season, we met Green Bay again. We should have taken them, but they beat us by a score of 21-20. We outplayed them, but they won. Everybody called it a moral victory because we outplayed them without Jim Brown. Nonsense! There is only one kind of victory in pro football—*scoreboard victory*.

The only possible good that I have ever seen in defeat is that it should indicate the weaknesses and what it takes to win the next time. It is important to remember that if a defeat in football, or in any other area of life, is magnified all out of proportion, it is likely to produce a defeatist attitude. This is damaging and will result in future failures. In pro football, recovery from defeat must involve more than merely swallowing one's pride—it must generate a determination to correct weaknesses and get in there and fight with a will to win.

Wrong attitudes produce a losing way

You've heard of the *winning way* in football. Well, a team can develop a *losing way* just as easily as a winning way. Defeat is tragic if it results in a loss of confidence—the first step on the losing way.

When you lose, the opposing players often slap you on the back and tell you what a great game you played even in defeat. This is supposed to be good sportsmanship. But, it can also be a subtle form of brainwashing.

In 1966 when we lost the first St. Louis game, one of their players came up to Ross Fichtner and said, "Now you guys go knock some people off for us." They had counted us out of the race, and we were actually only one-half game behind. Blanton Collier commented: "That's like trying to bury you with your eyes open."

The Green Bay game was the hardest to lose

Since we had been beaten by Green Bay in the 1965 championship game, we were really out to make amends when we played the Packers in 1966. They had humiliated us in every way a team could be humiliated. We should have beaten them this time, but we didn't, and the sportswriters in the Cleveland area came up with that "moral victory" business. Immediately after the game I had a speaking engagement in a local church. It was around 8:30 P.M. when this was over, and my ribs were really hurting, so I dropped by the clinic to have them x-rayed. Then Mavis and I went out to dinner, and it was midnight before we got home.

I couldn't sleep because of my sore ribs. They were giving me fits. But in addition, I was replaying the game in my mind. Eventually I fell asleep, but in just three or four hours I was rudely

Cleveland vs. Green Bay. Glass tackling Paul Hornung.

Blanton Collier instructs Frank Ryan, quarterback, Cleveland Browns.

Defensive end Bill Glass (80) tackles Bart Starr (15), quarterback, Green Bay Packers.

awakened by the alarm. As I rolled out of bed, a cloud of gloom enveloped me again. We'd lost when we should have won—and I ached all over.

Struggling into my clothes, I asked myself how I could have been so dumb as to accept two high school assembly speaking engagements for that day. If we had won, I would have enjoyed it, but now, I felt like trying to find a hole to hide in rather than face two large high school audiences. The schools were located in Alliance, Ohio, an hour and a half from home. I made the two speeches, and the enthusiasm of the high schoolers gave me a bit of a pickup. They didn't seem to think any less of me because we had lost, but I was still being hard on myself.

When I finally got to bed that Monday night, I was really beat. The ribs had quit hurting a little, and I slept like a log. I woke up the next morning feeling great. Somehow, I had forgotten that we had lost the big one—but then it dawned on me, and the old funeral feeling returned. I felt just like there had been a death in the family. It took a long time to get over that one.

After defeat, the coaches really have their work cut out for them
One mark of a good coach is in the way he deals with a team after a loss—especially when the team has played poorly. Blanton Collier does a good job in such situations. After losing two in a row to Green Bay and St. Louis in 1966, we were all prepared for the worst when Blanton came in on Tuesday. But he simply said, "Now we just pick up the pieces and go on from here." He picked us up by saying precisely the right thing: "We have the team to win, with or without Jim Brown."

Blanton would never admit that the team was any weaker after Jim quit. "This is the best team we've ever had," he would always say. After the season was over, we all had to admit that it wasn't the loss of Jim Brown that hurt us. We had a good running game without him.

Attitude comes primarily from the players

Every team I have ever played on has had at least one player who was a good picker-upper. Paul Wiggin is the best I've ever seen. He played defensive end on the opposite end of the line from me, and I wouldn't trade him for anybody. He's just a natural optimist. If anyone asked Paul about the team's attitude, he would instantly reply, "Great!" It didn't matter if we were all dragging the ground; Paul refused to believe it. With players like that around, you can't stay down long. But then, who can afford to stay down? There's always another game coming up— at most, only six days away.

One game at a time

I'm sure that defeat hurts me as deeply as anyone. But you can be sure that in spite of what the coaches and the team leaders do, each one of us has his own formula for getting over defeat.

Personally, I try to employ the old philosophy of forgetting what has happened in the past and concentrate my attention on the future. "One game at a time" is a well-worn football cliché, but it still works for me after about twenty-four hours of the bitter taste of defeat.

This idea is expressed in the Bible in the words of Paul: "Forgetting those things which are behind . . . I press toward the mark for the prize of the high calling of God in Christ Jesus." This helps me tremendously. With this thought in mind after a defeat, I regain my shattered faith in myself and in my teammates, knowing that next Sunday I'll need faith in both.

Defeat and the sportswriters

We are urged constantly by the coaches not to discuss defeats with the sportswriters. They seem to have a special talent for sinking their needles a little deeper immediately after a lost game, and they are anxious to know how you feel about the opposing team.

It is wise to say very little at this time to the run-of-the-mill sportswriter. Some of them can be trusted to use their discretion, but there is always the danger of being misquoted. Then too, there is the danger of saying something in an emotional moment that you would not want to see in print.

The emotions and attitudes of defeat in pro football are best quickly forgotten, so it is wise not even to verbalize them.

Part 4
The Challenge
of Preparation

10

Reporting Back to Training Camp

How I love the off-season! It's always a busy time for me, but I especially enjoy being with my wife Mavis, our two boys, and our little girl. Much of my off-season time is spent in speaking to high school and college student bodies, youth rallies, and weekend church meetings. This involves an average of two hundred engagements each year.

I live two distinct lives

I'm fortunate in being able to spend six months on my speaking schedule and six months in pro football. In a way, these two halves of my life are literally poles apart. But there's also a way in which each is merely an extension of the other. It seems to me that being a Christian means to live Christ daily in all of life, wherever we are. So, I believe that my football is as distinctly a Christian vocation as preaching before a Sunday morning congregation. Football gives me a greater opportunity to share my faith, and my faith gives me an inner strength and motivation for football that I wouldn't have otherwise.

Bill Glass speaking on national television, Billy Graham Crusade, Denver, Colorado.

avis and Bill Glass at home.

Billy Glass in his father's shoulder pads, shoes, and sweat suit.

The Glass family—Mindy, Mavis, Bobby, Bill, and Billy.

It's hard to get back into the harness

Each year it seems a little harder to get back in shape again, and it is infinitely more difficult to leave my Texas home and friends. Occasionally, I've taken my wife and children to Cleveland with me and put them in an apartment or house near the training camp so I can check on them. But the rigorous work and close scheduling of training camp makes this increasingly impractical. So, the separation from the family for the six weeks in training camp makes it tough to leave.

We begin to dread it about a month before the mid-July Friday that I have to leave, but mixed with the dread is the exhilaration of the challenge of another football year. Leaving Mavis adds to the pain of going; she makes our home a heaven on earth with her great attitude and her happy outlook. She has difficulty hiding her feelings from me, and sooner or later I say, "Okay, what's wrong?" She looks at me out of those beautiful eyes and responds, "I don't want you to leave us." Tears are in her eyes, and they'd be in mine too if I weren't too big to cry.

Leaving Waco is the hard part

The day always comes. The house is a regular beehive of activity. In addition to Mavis and the children, the farewell party is always swelled by my mother and my sister Linda—she's like my own daughter since she's twelve years younger than I am, and dad died when she was two. Then occasionally, a group of friends drops by for a final farewell. So, off I go in a shower of kisses and "be careful driving" instructions. Everyone is in tears except me, but as I said, I'm too big to cry, even though I really want to.

I haven't been on the highway very long before my thoughts move into the future. I'm determined to do a good job this year for the Browns. "We must win it this year."

Report day is a time of conflicting emotions

During those last miles through the beautiful rolling hills of

Ohio to the tiny town of Hiram, where our training camp is located, I get the same feeling year after year. It goes something like this: "Here I am again—same song, twelfth verse. When I get out of the car and lug my bags up to the dorm, I'll be caught up in a whirlwind of activities that will engulf me in a strange world for six months." It is a world that's vastly different from the spring and summer when the focus is on my work as a lay minister, standing before congregations who are listening for a word of hope. It is a world of concentration on a goal that will become the obsession of from forty to fifty people—players, coaches, and management—who visualize a world championship and direct every energy toward that goal. It is an intense world, characterized by vigorous and rough bodily contact; it is the world that produces the most popular sporting event in American history—pro football.

The same questions always haunt me at this time: Can this be real? Can I live in these two worlds, so vastly different, and through it all find that I belong to both? Am I pleasing to God in both lives? Does God really want me to enter this strange, rough world composed of obsessions seemingly far from the Christian ideal?

"God must be in favor of this," I always convince myself. "Here I am, and I wouldn't have such a feeling of oughtness if it weren't so." But to be perfectly honest, there is the lingering doubt and the soul-searching question, "Is this God's will for my life?" Possibly in another year or so I'll be sure—but of course, the assurance will be retroactive since I can't expect to play football forever. I've never been one hundred percent sure about anything except my marriage. Everything else, including football, has been about eighty percent "yes" and twenty percent "I don't know."

But the fifteen hundred mile trip is finally over, and I am catapulted into the rough world of football. And I always have a kind of quiet assurance that this is where I belong.

Why play football?

Can a man be a Christian and a roughneck in the oil fields at the same time? Can a man be a Christian and a soldier at the same time? Can a man be a Christian and play professional football? I say "yes," and possibly that's why I am here—just to prove it.

Actually, more is involved than that. I want to do what I enjoy doing and be a witness at the same time. I'm not interested in being a legalist, a moral policeman, or a stand-up preacher where it would be resented, but I do want to be a subtle witness to the fact that God is with me. Certainly, I want to avoid giving the impression to the pro football world that I think I'm infallible or that I'm better than the rank and file in a behavioral sense. On the other hand, I do want to point out that God is no stranger to any situation and that He lives in a man's heart in the midst of obsessions with earthly goals.

Professional football is a powerful force in American life. People spend more time in front of television watching football games than they do in church. It is this fact that gives me opportunities to witness that would otherwise not be open.

People still feel that a minister ought to be different

There are many dedicated Christians in pro football, but my case is a bit different from most of them. While I'm not ordained, I am a lay minister. I was fortunate in being able to complete my seminary education by devoting all of my time in resident study in six years of off-season time. I enjoyed my studies, and I encountered many authentic Christians among my professors and fellow students.

But out of all this, the thing most discouraging to me was the change in attitude of my teammates when I went to seminary. I was treated differently. They seemed bent on trying to force me to be a moral policeman. While I was perfectly willing to be an example and wanted to live by a high moral standard, I didn't want to become a guardian of other people's morals.

Back to a world of conflicting feelings

Now, to be perfectly honest with you, all of my feelings on returning to camp are not exhilarating. For nearly ten years I have been trying to fight and win a battle of emotions. Sometimes I think I have it made, and I feel completely at one with the entire group of players—both those who live, talk, and think clean as well as those who do not. Then at other times, I give way to feelings of rejection. Even when I play my heart out for the team and make the supreme effort, there are times when I have the feeling of not being accepted. This has caused me a great deal of concern because I want my fellow players to accept me as a football player and as a person—even as I want to accept and respect them as persons. But as I have attempted to analyze it, I have come to believe that they are reacting not to what I am, but to what they think I am, because of the stereotype of the legalistic religion that is loaded with "thou shalt nots." What they are rejecting is an *image* of Christianity —an image *I do not embrace*.

Through my own attitudes of acceptance and honesty, I must help them to see and understand that God is not a thief who would rob life of its excitement and make it flat to the taste. God is not an insipid kill-joy. He is a God of love, and Christ has come to give us a rich and full life. Unfortunately, Christianity has come to be characterized by a narrow legalism.   .

It's always good to be back

There's no doubt about it, it's always good to see the fellows again after being separated for six months. You can't live through the things we live through together and not have an esprit de corps—these were my buddies all right.

Not that you like all of the guys, far from it—some are really irritating in little egotistical ways, in uncouth habits, or in just plain littleness. But, that's just one part of it . . . you do have a family feeling for the whole gang, and you learn to love them in spite of the irritating things.

Loneliness sets in early

There is always a lot of backslapping, handshaking, and good-natured horseplay as we all come together again. This is a great bunch of guys, and this year we are going to show everybody that Cleveland has the greatest team in the world. But in the midst of all the fun and noise, there is a lump in my throat. While I've only been separated from the family for a few hours, it seems much longer. How I miss Mavis, the boys, and little Mindy. That fifteen hundred miles back to Texas seems like an unbearable barrier. But I've lived through it before, and I'll just have to make it again. After training season Mavis will be moving the kids to Cleveland, so I'll see them in a little over a month.

The action begins with roll call

Report day has arrived. It starts out with roll call at 12:15 P.M., followed by the physicals, and we get the works: blood samples, urinalyses, electrocardiograms, etc. I weigh in at two hundred and fifty-eight pounds—just five or six pounds off my best playing weight. All the guys appear to be in shape, but the first workout will tell the story, a story we all know by heart. Looks are deceiving. The little exercise programs we had followed during off-season just wouldn't compensate for the soft living. We'll soon see how out of shape we really are.

At 4:00 P.M. we come together in the big meeting room. Collier puts it right on the line just like we knew he would. He was disappointed that we booted the big one last year—we'd won in our division and then lost to the Dallas Cowboys. He wasn't happy and neither were we, because we each felt in our hearts we should have won it.

After the first training camp meal at 6:00 P.M. we settle down to watch last year's highlights film. And then just as we expected, Blanton says, "Now I want you to forget last year. It's this year we've got to think about now."

It has been a long day, a happy day, and a sad day—a day of conflicting emotions.

11

Press Day

They call it Press Day—I'd call it lecture day. It starts at 9:00 A.M. when Blanton Collier opens up with his "State of the Browns" address. It all depends on the situation whether the opening is gloomy or gleeful; Collier is a psychologist by nature, and he picks his attitude to fit the need as he sees it.

The atmosphere depends on how we finished last year
The year after we beat the Baltimore Colts for the 1964 World Championship, Collier opened the meeting by saying, "Well, the honeymoon is over." He was referring to the six months of dreaming we had just concluded during the off-season—dreaming about beating Baltimore. When we came back after being mauled by Green Bay in the mud of the 1965 championship game, Collier said, "Well, now the funeral is over." Six months of reliving the horrors of that Green Bay game were finally coming to an end. He expected us to forget that game and get with it for the new season.

Blanton usually asserts vehemently, "You guys have got to believe you can win. You have control over what you think—

make it a positive attitude. What you think and feel about our football team is more important than your physical ability. If you think right, progress and success will follow, and together we can accomplish anything."

Some things you hear over and over

But there are certain things you can always expect. For one thing, he'll always say, "There are some people who predict that we'll finish in the second half of our division." Then he growls, "But I for one don't expect to be buried before I stop breathing and close my eyes."

Then we always get the routine about playing one game at a time: "There are fourteen objectives. But we've got to think of one at a time. No, we can't win them all—don't even think about that—instead think about those Redskins [or the team we are playing in the first league game, whoever it may be]. Don't think about results, just give it your best; give it all the enthusiasm and dedication at your command." These are simple, basic truths, but there is value in repeating them. It is essential that we apply them in a practical way rather than let them roll off like water off a duck's back. That's part of staying young mentally rather than becoming senile.

What Collier's like

Blanton Collier is a great person and an excellent coach. He's not a genius. He doesn't have super intelligence, but he does have unbelievable dedication. He starts early in the morning during training camp with a 7:30 breakfast. He's with his assistants working on plans for the day until 9:10, and then he goes down to dress for our workout. At about 9:28 he walks into the briefing room. He spends those two minutes diagramming plays on the board or talking with some individual player about a point he should work on. At 9:30 he turns his attention to the team, who by now are sitting quietly in full-dress uniform waiting for his brief lecture or for the word to hit the practice field. We are on

Coach Blanton Collier of the Cleveland Browns illustrates blocking techniques.

the practice field until 11:00. After supervising our workout, Blanton has stacks of phone calls to be made, daily press conferences, and daily meetings with quarterbacks and coaches. Every minute not already filled by routine things—two workouts and a night meeting—is taken up in Collier's long day. There are always trades to be made, owners to be informed, assistant coaches to be consulted, encouraged, or instructed. His days are filled to overflowing, and he is usually at his desk until late at night devising new ways to make the Browns a winner.

Coaching is a real tough job in the NFL

The assistant coaches usually meet somewhere for some brief diversion each night at 9:00 following the squad meeting. When some of us leave at 9:00 to go to Garretsville for our nightly meeting of the "coffee club," Blanton is at his desk hard at work, and he's still there when we return around 10:30.

On some nights we see the entire coaching staff in his room. They go on and on and on—hashing and rehashing defense and offense, plays and players, cuts and trades, practices and games. As training camp progresses the players have less physical work and even less meeting time, but the coaches work harder and harder. They work almost around the clock at times. And when the training camp is over and the season begins, the pressure mounts.

You can see why Blanton commands respect, and even though you may be a twelve-year veteran and have heard his "State of the Browns" message several times before, you know that this man is as sincere as the days are long. And they are mighty long for him.

I guess the toughest job a coach has is to cut a player. Sometimes it's even harder when the guy has a wife and kids, or when he came to camp with fanfare. The player may have left his little hometown like a conquering hero, but he has to return as a failure. Collier is sincere when he says that cutting is the most distasteful job he has.

Cutting is handled in as painless a manner as possible. No big explanations, no condemnations. The cut has to come, and it does come early to the players who just don't have a chance. It takes longer with the borderline cases.

Blanton always concludes his "State of the Browns" address with a word about individual improvement. "The team can't improve unless the individual improves," Collier reiterates. "Everyone must concentrate on what he is doing wrong and then work individually to correct his weaknesses." But this is only part one of a two-part episode. Following a ten minute break, we are back in our chairs shortly after ten o'clock.

Second meeting of training camp comes at 10:00 A.M. on Monday

At our second meeting, Collier always gives us our daily schedule. It doesn't vary much from one season to another. We always have two-a-day workouts for the first two weeks. These are usually from 9:30 to 11:00 in the mornings and from 3:00 to 4:30 in the afternoons. Individual work to iron out the wrinkles follows the team workout. We have lunch at noon and supper at 6:00 P.M. Our one scheduled meeting of the day is held at 7:00 P.M. and lasts about two hours.

So, we have about two hours to kill after the evening meeting until bedtime at 11:00. And we definitely have a curfew at training camp. We've got to be in the dorm at 11:00 P.M. regardless.

There's not much time for diversion at training camp. We can drive the four miles to Garretsville for coffee before bedtime, but there's not time for anything else. Garretsville is a typical little town of about five thousand people with a barber shop, a drugstore, hardware store, several shops, cleaners, washateria, and a main drag. There's also a cafe where the "coffee club" meets.

We usually have the rule book thrown at us

The second meeting usually deals with our relationship to Hiram College, where we hold our training camp. We are told where to park our cars, to stay away from the college girls, and to dress properly at all times. Our lecture covers everything from table manners to drinking. In short, we are urged to guard the pro football image. Although we're grown men and most of us are married and have families, we all realize that there have to be rules. If we break them, we get it in the pocketbook—we are fined. When Paul Brown was head coach, he would announce bluntly, "There'll be no smoking or drinking." Any who did it, did it secretly, careful not to let him catch them. Brown was a strict disciplinarian and demanded that his players act with class. And for years in dress, in table manners, in grooming, in conduct, and in winning on the field, the Browns were the class of the league. When Blanton became head coach, he relaxed the rules somewhat.

It seems to me that it is a mistake to tell grown men that they can't drink or smoke. I don't smoke or drink, but I think that rules prohibiting such things are useless. Blanton always says, "If you must smoke or drink, don't do it publicly because of the bad example to the youth of America."

Pictures and more pictures

Picture-taking time is 2:00 P.M. We get into uniform and go through a simulated workout. Reporters, radio, and television people are everywhere. They want action pictures, stills in groups, and individual shots.

The main workout at this picture-taking session consists of running the forty-yard dash. And this is for the record, too. It's mighty important to run these dashes as fast as you can because judgments are made about your condition from your time. If your forty-yard dash time stays about the same every year, you are all right; but if it gets slower each season, it becomes a factor in your retirement. Five seconds flat is about the best a big lineman can be expected to do. I practice dashes for several weeks before report day to be sure I am ready. And so does almost everyone on the team.

Another lecture at 4:00 P.M.

After the pictures and the dashes, along with some loosening up exercises, we are back to the salt mines again. This time the lecture is usually inspirational in tone.

"Brains share equal billing with muscle in the game of professional football," Collier leads off. He has the full attention of the team, although the old pros like Lou Groza have heard these opening lectures for nearly twenty years from either Paul Brown or Blanton. Collier emphasizes dedication, concentration, and confidence. He talks about the first exhibition game, how ready the opposition is going to be, and how badly they want to beat the Browns. Everybody seems to want to beat the Browns. He concludes, "With team effort and determination, I believe you can hurdle each challenge. I believe it, and I expect you to believe it."

Dinner dispositions run the gamut from ecstatic to suicidal

It is hard to predict how the atmosphere will be at the evening meal on Press Day. Everybody is secretly wondering if he can make it again this year—will he be great success or a flop?

Some of the guys whoop it up to hide their feelings of insecurity. The rookies usually eat quietly at tables off to themselves. To everyone, training camp looks like a long hard drag, and some of us wonder: "Maybe we should have retired this year after all."

But with food so good, it's easy to get a lift in spirits. And then, it is good to be back—yes, it's going to be a great year for the Browns.

At 7:00 P.M. *we see the highlights from last year*

On the first night, we see the highlights film of last year. The whole message of the day is, "You did all right last year, but you can do better this year. And we expect you to do better. In fact, we must win it all."

Believe me, the sack looks good to all of us after Press Day.

Even though we haven't done a lot of physical work, it's very tiring. So you hit the sack. And it seems like you could sleep a week. But you just lie there. The excitement of everything is just too much. Seeing everybody again and getting back into uniform for the first time in six months, plus the challenge of a new season really gets the adrenalin all charged up.

Some of the fellows take sleeping pills for the first few nights. It takes a while to settle down, that's for sure.

"God help me to play the game and live in training camp to Your glory."

12

The First Day

The first day of two-a-day workouts is always tough. As a rule, you haven't slept much the night before, or, if you took sleeping pills, you feel groggy. At best, you are nervous about it all. The same old question haunts the veteran, "Am I still up to this tough life?" To the rookie, it's even more a morning of insecurity. He is hounded by the big throbbing question, "Can I really make it in the pros?" He knows that many college greats have been flunk-outs in the pros. Some of the veterans overcome this nervousness by being loud and overly friendly, while the rookies are usually quiet and apologetic.

Some are slow starters in the mornings

The early morning schedule is not too demanding. You can get up early if you are geared that way, or you can stay in the sack until 8:45 A.M. If you do stay that long, it is a hurry-up deal all the way. There's just time to grab a cup of coffee and a sweet roll before rushing to the training room in order to be fully dressed in uniform and in your seat in the briefing room by 9:27, and ready to hit the field at 9:30.

Before going out to the practice field, Blanton tells us just what we are going to accomplish the first day. This is really it—no pictures, no sportswriters—just plain hard work and football.

First we do calisthenics

Following the briefing, we run down through a tunnel and out onto the lush green playing field, located in the beautiful rolling hill country of northern Ohio.

But this is no time to enjoy the scenery, although I'm sure that the several hundred spectators who are always present enjoy it. There's work ahead for us, and everyone has kind of a no-nonsense attitude.

Our first action consists of calisthenics for the whole team. The calisthenics are led by a different coach every day. Eddie Ulinski usually has the job the first day. "Ully" is by far the toughest of the coaches in leading calisthenics. He is a nice guy and takes a lot of good-natured ribbing. But he takes his job seriously and gives us the long count on every exercise. Ully yells, "Readiiiee, ooone, twooo, three, four." And a chorus comes back from the players, "readiiiee Ullieee."

The next day "The Hawk" leads in calisthenics. Bob Nussbaumer picked up this nickname at Detroit, where he was a talent scout for years. He earned the name "The Hawk" because of his ability to hawk talent. I first met him when I played in the Senior Bowl game my last year in college. I was Detroit's first draft choice, and they were trying hard to sign me. "The Hawk" was there with Nick Kerbiway and Buster Ramsey. Kerbiway was a silver-tongued orator who droned on for hours as to why I should play for Detroit. Nussbaumer, Ramsey, and I were his audience in that Mobile hotel room, but I finally decided to go play in Canada. I was *persona non grata* with Detroit because they'd wasted their top draft choice on me. But I returned to the States and played for Detroit the next year. Anyway, he came to the Browns as a coach three years after I was traded to Cleveland. So, we're back together on the same ball club, and Hawk leads the calisthenics to an occasional "squawk" like a hawk.

Next, it's Howard Brinker's day, and he looks like a puppet on a string while leading calisthenics. When he does the Jumping Jack or hop straddling exercise, he bounces so high that it looks comical and evokes a lot of good-natured comments from the players.

Nick Skorich follows Howard, and he demands so much respect that only the most daring venture to suggest that he looks like a service station gas pump. Nick is short and stocky. It's really surprising that he isn't ribbed more because he's constantly ribbing someone. While trotting by the offensive drills with his defensive line, he'll say, "You guys get to work; we're tired of carrying you on our backs." Then he'll turn around and say to us, "You've heard of the Fearsome Foursome at L.A. We're the Fearful Foursome at Cleveland." One time he told me, "You're in the wrong sport; you should be in baseball. Just think you'd have ten no-hitters going for you" (referring to his constantly emphasized point of my not hitting hard enough).

During calisthenics the players form straight lines according to position. Defensive backs, linebackers, lineman, offensive backs, receivers, guards, and tackles each have a separate line. There are seven lines, and your place in the line is determined by seniority.

The player who has been in the league the longest is first in line, and so on down to the rookies. I started out six years ago with the Browns and was at the end of the line, but I've been working my way to the front. Bob Gain retired first, then Dick Modzelewski (he's now our defensive line coach). Now that Paul Wiggin has retired, I lead our line. Man, does that make me feel old! Just think, I'm at the front of the seniority line for the defensive linemen and not far back on the whole club. It seems just like yesterday when I was trying to break in as a rookie.

After about fifteen minutes of calisthenics, we break up and report to the seven groups I mentioned before. For me, of course, that means the defensive line. For the last couple of years, rather than go through our regular calisthenic routine, we work out on the Exer-Genie—an exercise machine that supposedly warms you up and strengthens you.

We start out with a big squad

During the season, we carry six defensive linemen—four regulars and two substitutes. However, during the training camp period, we often have as many as ten or twelve including the rookies. We start out by drilling in four-man units, with the starters working together. With twelve players, we can have three of these groups going through the same drills alternately. The right to be on that first unit is important.

If a player is customarily on the first unit and is taken off for some reason, he is usually very disturbed, although he may have enough poise not to show it. Sometimes the players get so frustrated that fights break out during scrimmage or during the first rough drill. Others manage to control themselves but do everything possible to get back on that starting unit. They think of it constantly, they dream of it, they work for it, and they talk about it. The gripes often sound like this: "Tell me honestly, do you think I'm getting a fair shake?" or, "I know I can play somewhere in this league," or "I wish they'd trade me."

It's good to have some extra rookies

At this stage we are usually glad to see an odd number of linemen turn out. You see, if there are eleven, it means that we work out in two groups, with three substitutes to spell us from time to time. Believe me, you really appreciate those rest breaks on the first day of practice. None of us is in peak condition. It seems that no matter how hard you work at getting ready for those first days of training camp, you are never in good enough shape. It's hard to push yourself as much as the coach pushes you.

The sounds and smells trigger the emotions

With all the anxiety of the first day, there are some deep down thrills, too. For one thing, you are exhilarated by the sounds and the smells around you. The sounds of the coaches hollering and the signal-calling stirs up the blood of an old pro.

And, believe it or not, the smell of new equipment is almost as good as the smell of a new car. Unfortunately, new equipment is usually hot and sticky and isn't as comfortable as it will be when it is cured by mud and sweat. The hardest pieces of equipment to break in are new helmets. They are uncomfortable and rub you raw. It usually takes about a month to get a helmet to the comfortable stage. But I still like all of the sounds and smells after over twenty years in football.

Then comes the individual effort

After the unit drills, we go to the fundamentals. We usually start off with stance, form, and position. The coaches are especially anxious at this time about stance and form.

We have several drills where we hit the dummy. First of all, we get into our stance and "fire off" the line as fast as possible and hit the dummy as hard as we can.

Next, we work on the fundamentals of defensive line play. This involves two basic things, "hitting and locating." The coaches are especially strong on this and for good reason. If you hit an opposing lineman and bury yourself (get your head down or arms tangled so you can't see or move well), you may overpower him, but that isn't enough. You must not only play the opposing lineman, you have to play the ball. The offensive lineman opposite you is instructed to "tie you up" (occupy you so you can't make the tackle) so the runner can pierce the forward wall and break into the secondary. So, the opposition is satisfied to get bowled over if in so doing they can tie you up and keep you from making the play.

The idea is to "hit and locate." That means hit the opponent and control him so he doesn't get "head position" on you (get his head between you and the ball carrier). When you have him controlled, you get your head up, locate the ball, and move toward it. If the play is off tackle, you've got to slide to the point of attack where the ball is coming and get your arms and shoulder into the runner as he tries to break through the hole his linemen have gouged out for him.

We have creative coaches

Obviously, closing your eyes or burying your head like an ostrich into the stomach of the opponent eliminates you from the play. Our coaches have rigged up an ingenious arrangement on our seven-man sled. They have several flags controlled by ropes. When the flags move, we are supposed to hit our man (one of the dummies on the sled); but with the movement of the coach's hat, we are to release and pursue to the right or left as he indicates. In one hand the coach holds the rope that activates the flags to set us off, and in the other hand he holds the cap that he uses to signal the direction of our pursuit.

There are different ways to charge in the line

There are many ways to hit and still allow yourself freedom to slide off and make the tackle on the ball carrier, or slide off and get through to the passer. First, we practice a simple right forearm and shoulder charge. Then we practice a left forearm charge, springing off of it to the next dummy with a right forearm charge which simulates a game situation where you may be double teamed.

We practice this basic fundamental of hitting and locating the ball, of hitting and sliding right or left as the play seems to be developing. During training the coach gives us the signal to slide either right or left, but in an actual game situation it is the opposing ball carrier that gives us the cue for action.

On some drills where we work individually, we may hit as many as four dummies in succession on the seven-man sled. In this drill we hit the first and bounce back about two yards and

Defensive line coach Nick Skorich illustrates a point to Jim Kanicki, defensive tackle, and Bill Glass at Cleveland practice field. Note the size of Kanicki's arm and shoulders.

then hit the next dummy with a forearm and shoulder. We bounce back and fire into the third dummy and then into the fourth. The object is to learn to hit and move quickly. It is important to be able to hit a blocker, shed him, and then make the tackle. The power with which we attack the dummies on this drill is unbelievable. Jim Kanicki hits them the hardest of any man on the team. He has the biggest arms and shoulders of anyone in the NFL. It sounds like a shotgun when he hits the dummy. Bystanders are amazed at the power of this defensive giant.

Back to defensive unit work

After this contact work with the dummies, we usually line up in a four-man defensive unit and run our defensive plays, popping off the line and hitting an imaginary opposing lineman and moving laterally in the direction indicated by the way Dick Modzelewski, our defensive line coach, moves his hat. This is done so that we can learn our particular individual assignments on defense.

It may seem to spectators in the stands as if every man is playing it by ear—charging any way he chooses in a hit and miss fashion. But we have our special assignments, and there is a zone in which we operate with first and second responsibilities. There is a primary responsibility for a player on every defense, and it must be covered at all cost. Then you react to your secondary responsibility. You pursue and help your teammates—every defense has its weakness and strength, and you must be able to identify them.

If every man "played his own" on every down of every game, few yards would be made. "Playing your own," means just doing your job in order of importance, remembering first, second, and third responsibilities and doing these things in order.

When we were kids, we used to play games where we would take turns doing this or that. You don't take turns in pro football. There's teamwork all right, but if the play is in your zone, you don't stand back and wait.

I remember one particular game while I was at Detroit. Three of our backs and I had a runner hemmed in on the sidelines, and each of us was expecting one of the others to make the tackle. We were all "waiting on Joe" to make the tackle. Needless to say, Joe didn't arrive, the ball carrier scored, and we lost the game. You can imagine what fools we thought we were. In the film session a teammate ribbed us by saying, "You go first. No after you, No, after you." You have to be aggressive in pro football.

Of course, we all know that at times you will be unable to carry out your assignments because you may be flat on your back when you ought to have the quarterback flat on his back. The opposition is getting paid to do its job, too. You have to practice the assignments just the way they are supposed to work out. You've always got about seven men there facing you across the line of scrimmage whose assignment is to see that you don't carry out yours. But that's football.

Team drills

After about fifteen minutes of these defensive drills, the whole team comes together for a dummy scrimmage. While we've been doing our drills, the backs have been running plays for timing, defensive backs have been working on agility drills, and receivers have been busy on running and pass catching drills or on hitting the dummies. They don't hit the dummies very hard because most of them aren't very big, and they don't think of this as being very important. As a rule, the receivers hit the dummies on the other side of the same seven-man sled the defensive linemen use.

One day we were grunting and pounding the dummy for everything we were worth when "The Hawk" (Coach Bob Nussbaumer) came up with the receivers. They started pecking away on the other side of the blocking sled. The contrast of the receivers' tapping on the dummies with the big boom of the defensive linemen was comical. "Mo" (Dick Modzelewski) looked around at them and said, "Now come on, guys, you've got to be kidding; you don't call that blocking, do you?" Everybody had a good laugh. But, there's no laughing when they start sprinting out like race horses and make those great catches in passing drills. We've got some of the best receivers in football on our team.

The offense is busy too

In the meantime, the offensive line runs through all sorts of blocking drills. The defensive backs and the receivers usually go through about a fifteen or twenty minute passing drill before team play (dummy scrimmage with the total team working together.) This occupies roughly the last third of our ninety minute workout.

Both the offense and the defense run through the plays without any heavy contact. This is obviously better for the offense than the defense. They have a good chance to polish up their plays, but we know the plays so well that we have an advantage in defending against them. But on the other hand, if they can run successfully against us, they'll do well against the opposition who are not as familiar with our plays.

Naturally, the opposition has good scouting and is going to know pretty well what our offense will run. The point is, the offense must make their plays work for yardage against a defense that knows exactly what they're going to do. They've got to do it so well that it will overcome all opposition. So, in dummy scrimmage we must make a hard, fast charge and then ease off and let them block us, so they can get their timing down.

After workout, special work for a few minutes

After workout, Blanton usually gets us together in the middle of the field and tells us to take care of any blisters or small injuries. Everybody is encouraged to stay on an additional ten or fifteen minutes for extra work on individual weaknesses.

Each man works on his specialty. To give the linemen extra work, they have us run back the field goals that Lou Groza or Dan Cockroft kick. Sometimes, just to get a little extra running, some of us linemen join the passing drill. It doesn't take but a few patterns to get my fill of being a pass receiver. The defensive line always does some running, usually about six fifty-yard dashes at about two-thirds speed. A few of the linemen stay after workout to hit the dummy, while the passers and receivers stay out and throw passes and work on patterns.

Resting after first workout

On this first morning of workouts, we're hot and tired. So we trot off the field, back through the tunnel, up the long steps, and into the dressing room where we tank up on cool water and ice. After taking a shower and cooling off a bit, we head for our dormitory rooms. Usually, we go by way of the dining hall and get a soft drink.

Mail is a big thing at training camp. We really look forward to it. There is a short time for reading and relaxing before the noon meal. Sometimes we go to our rooms and lie in bed to read mail or the paper, or we may just sit and read in the meeting room adjoining the cafeteria. This has us close to the door of the dining room and the front of the chow line.

Afternoon workout time comes much too soon

After lunch, we're free until about two o'clock, when it is time to head back to the dressing room, get dressed, and be ready to hit the practice field again by three o'clock. Those workouts come so often that it seems like all you are doing is dressing, showering, and redressing. By the time one workout is over, you are getting ready for another.

Following the afternoon workout, some of us do isometrics and weight lifting—then shower, dress, pick up our valuables, and we're off to check the mail, read the paper, and stand in line for a huge dinner at six.

Our night meeting starts at seven o'clock. First, we meet as a group; then we break up into offense and defense; then into even smaller groups with offensive backs, receivers, and linemen meeting with their individual coaches. The defense breaks into two groups: linebackers and backs in one, and linemen in the other.

Then by nine or a little before, we are free to do what we like until eleven. Some of the players go to the Garretsville coffee club and some go for stronger refreshment. Others just hang around the dorm and watch TV, study their play books, read, or write letters. I usually go down to the Garretsville coffee club (about eight to twelve players in the group). Curfew comes at eleven. There's always a bed check, so we're careful to be in on time.

13

The Veterans vs. The Rookies

When I was a rookie at Detroit, the veterans gave us a bad time. My biggest problem was to keep the right mental attitude in spite of this. I knew the veterans weren't particularly eager for me to make the team because I'd have to beat out one of them or their friends to do so. There was a constant effort on their part to make me feel that I wasn't good enough to take any veteran's place. A twenty-one-year-old inexperienced rookie begins to feel that he's fighting an entire ball club.

There are several reasons why veterans put pressure on the rookie. With all the tension and frustration of training camp, there has to be some way to let off steam, so the poor rookie becomes the butt of every joke. He is kidded and needled good-naturedly. Usually this is all in fun and quite harmless, and it makes an otherwise dreary situation somewhat more bearable.

Jealousy raises its ugly head at times

A second reason for giving rookies a hard time is due to the fact that many of them are being paid considerably more than the veterans. It isn't so bad now that the leagues have merged and the high "bonus babies" are a thing of the past. When I went to Detroit, our pay was so small that this could hardly have caused any hard feelings. But the problem still exists, and although feelings are under control most of the time, occasionally some frustrations are vented in ways that are not just for fun.

The third big factor is fear

The really big concern of every rookie and veteran alike is the fear of sitting on the bench. Every pro football player wants in that game.

To illustrate, let's suppose that you are a veteran defensive lineman and that there is a good rookie breathing down your collar for your starting assignment. It's a tight race and you feel that the coach is torn between the two of you. Then one day you get in there in the heat of battle and make a hard tackle and hear an ankle pop. It hurts, but not too badly; you can hang in there and nobody would know about your injury. You know that you ought to get off the ankle for the sake of your future, and worse than that, you know that you are not really delivering. You can't fire off the line with that ankle. The offensive lineman is beating you on every play, not too badly, but he is beating you. Only you know about the injury, and you know why you are getting beat. The coach keeps thinking that maybe he should put the rookie in, but in deference to your record as an established pro, he keeps hoping you will start getting off the blocks sooner and get to that quarterback as you have throughout all your career.

You know deep down in your heart that you should take yourself out and let the rookie come in. They are making the short yardage plays on third down right through you. Maybe a sound-bodied rookie could help the team more than an injured veteran. It takes a real man to take himself out in a case like that; you wait and hope the coach will step in and do it for you—it'd be easier that way.

Hazing

Rookies are treated much better at Cleveland than we were at Detroit. During each meal we were told to stand up in a chair, hold our hands over our hearts, and sing our school song. For me it was *That Good Old Baylor Line*. That wasn't so bad —it was all in fun, even though we didn't think it was so funny at the time. It's a lot like being a freshman and having a bunch of pesky sophomores around having fun at your expense.

But, we also experienced some other discrimination. For instance, we had to ride in separate buses from the vets. Also, we had to get to the training room an hour and a half before workouts, in order to get taped and be out of the way before the vets came down. These two things are true with almost every team in the league. In fact, at Cleveland this is about all that the veterans demand of rookies.

At Detroit we were forced to put on a rookie show, which opened with a jockey strap-clad chorus line of rookies and closed with an act that made fun of the coaching staff. Bobby Lane, our quarterback, was the chief engineer of all rookie harassment at Detroit. His last year with Detroit was my first. Boy, I really caught it from him. He was tough on all rookies, but he really bore down on me. At that time I was playing offensive center, and I wasn't snapping the ball back to him exactly as he wanted. Then, he had heard I was studying to be a minister, and this seemed to challenge him to see what I was really made of.

I sang *That Good Old Baylor Line* at every meal, standing on my chair with my hand over my heart. The conclusion was always greeted by a round of boos led by Bobby. All of the other rookies got the same treatment.

But, Bobby was a real character. Just about the time you'd get to the point where you hated him, he'd pass out an offhand compliment. "Glass, you're not as bad a rookie as I thought you were going to be," he'd say. Also, he took Harley Sewell, Gil Mains, and me out on the night before our first league game against Baltimore for a big steak dinner and picked up the check. That, I never will forget. They told story after story, and I listened with rapt attention. They were especially delighted over my interest because evidently everyone else had heard their stories over and over again.

Last year, when the rookies had been in camp for a week, I was down the hall and heard one of the little defensive backs talking on the pay phone. As I walked toward him, he was saying: "No, I really can't tell how I'm doing. Well, at least I'm still around. [He'd survived the first cut, made after the first week.] Boy, it really is different. In fact, it's more different than I'd ever dreamed. There's so much to learn so fast. It's just tough every way you look at it."

Sometimes rookies are nice to have around

During the training camp days when none of us is in peak condition, the rookies are really nice to have around. You can be sure that during those hot, humid July and August days we're glad to share the work with the rookies. When we are scrimmaging, our coach watches us closely, and he'll pull us out and put in a rookie when the heat begins to get to us. Some players have more trouble with the heat than others.

Jim Kanicki is almost like a polar bear. When it's cold, he feels great, but when it's hot, he gets muscle cramps and sometimes passes out. I remember the first time he really took the count was after a game with the Rams. It happened in the Los Angeles airport; he went down and it took half the team to get him into a wheel chair and off to the hospital.

During training camp scrimmages, the whole implication is that the rookie is being put in to give him some experience, not to give the veterans a rest. The coaches and the vets know that it is done for both reasons, but the rookie believes it is all for his benefit. Naturally, we would like for the rookies to think we are the original iron men, all muscle, and completely indestructible.

There's an old saying from baseball that goes like this: "Don't leave your glove on the mound too long; somebody will come along and pick it up." That's why a veteran doesn't mind a rest, but he doesn't want a rookie playing too long in his spot. He may get to liking it too well. But there's always room on any team for a hustling, hitting, aggressive rookie with the right attitude if he has any ability.

There's a lot of psychology in the vet-rookie relationship

There are some strange dynamics going on between veterans and rookies. To begin with, there's this sense of distrust and fear that the rookie is going to come up with your job. You can't discount that; it's really there. A lot of us talk loud: "Just let 'em try to replace me." We hope they don't find anyone better than we are, but, of course, the best way to keep this from happening is by working hard yourself.

The players who are roughest on the rookies are usually the ones who had a bad season the year before. They are fighting for their jobs, believing that they still have quite a few years of play ahead if they can hang on. Some of them are nursing bad knees or injuries that might spell the difference between their going or staying. You can't really blame them for feeling pretty dejected, and at times this may be expressed in discrimination against the rookies.

Then, there are the vets who are such lovers of football and of the team that they want to lend a helping hand to the rookies. These men have matured to the point that they're able to take in stride the fact that age catches up with everyone. The day is coming when they'll be watching these kids on television from an easy chair as they take their places in the lineup. So, to a large extent, the guys who are nicer to the rookies are the ones who have already decided on the date of their retirements. They are not fighting it.

Generally speaking, most of the vets are nice to the rookies. Maybe it's a genuine brand of sportsmanship that motivates

them. Or maybe it's that many of them have sons of their own
coming along, and they just naturally turn to youth in an
honest effort to help them grow up and become their best. The
majority of the veterans are warm-hearted guys who would go
out of their way to help anybody.

Paul Wiggin was an excellent example of this type of player.
He has always been friendly and helpful to every rookie, even
those who could possibly get his job. I've always marveled
at his unselfishness, but never more than in 1967 when Jack
Gregory, an outstanding college player, came to our team.
Jack was fast, had great balance, and seemed to have everything
necessary to be a great defensive end. To make matters worse,
Wiggin was playing in his eleventh season in the NFL, and at
thirty-three he was older than most men at that position in the
league. But, Paul helped Jack in every conceivable way. At
times I was sorry that I couldn't help Jack too, but what could
I add to what Paul was doing? He knows far more about playing or coaching than I do. Now he's gone to coach at San Francisco, and I wish my son could be coached by him—he's the
greatest.

Injuries can change personalities

The fear of injury hovers over every player in pro football.
It is probably hardest on the rookie. He feels he has it in him
to make it great, but an injury could spoil a whole lifetime for
him. Many a great college star misses his chance in the pros
because of an injury at the wrong moment. Without that injury he would have been great for many years; with it, he was
washed out for all time. The difference between greatness and
being cut is often an untimely injury.

Injuries are of two types: the aggravating type and the bad
ones. The first frustrates you, and the second sidelines you.
Those minor hurts can be really frustrating: You come up with
a groin strain and it has to be wrapped daily. It won't kill you,
but if you go out and play with it, it may give the other guy

just the break he needs to show the coach what he has. Eventually a little muscle strain could cost you your starting job.

Usually, you sweat out these muscle strains, blisters, shin splints, etc., acting as if they don't bother you at all even though they may be about to drive you crazy. During two seasons, I developed a very painful toe infection. It caused a big hole between my little toe and the one next to it. None of the doctors knew how to stop it. My teammates called it the jungle rot. Finally, a foot doctor gave me a tannic acid powder that dried it out.

Then, a couple of years ago I developed an excruciating pain in my foot, and the team doctor couldn't do anything to relieve it. I finally had to have the nerve removed. These little things don't keep you from playing, but they do hinder your effectiveness. I've never been hurt badly enough to miss a game because of injury. But I think the worst thing a player can do is to worry about getting hurt. I never consider that possibility. When a player starts worrying about injury, he takes his mind off his business. That causes him to let up and become even more susceptible to injury.

Here's the way it ought to be

It is unrealistic for a veteran really to like the rookie who is threatening his job security. Even so, there is no need for bad feelings or for the "needle," except in a kidding sort of way that everyone expects. On the playing field, it's every man for himself as far as his job is concerned.

But the social side of it is something else. There is a caste system in most training camps. The rookies stick together, and the vets stick together. When I was a rookie, I remember one of the veterans saying, "We don't want to get to like you too much, because then when you get cut we lose a friend."

14

Scrimmages

Scrimmages are serious business to the players, but they are shot through with a holiday atmosphere for the little town of Hiram, Ohio. Usually these full-speed contact scrimmages are held on Saturdays. Most years we have two of them before the exhibition season begins.

The quiet little college town is flooded with outsiders

We have two scrimmages on successive Saturdays. The Hiram Old-Timers from Hiram College sponsor one scrimmage, and the Touchdown Club sponsors the other scrimmage. Hiram is proud of the Browns and the part their town plays in preparing the team.

On Old-Timers Day the alumni of the small Hiram College return to campus. It is a colorful occasion with alumni meetings and a big banquet at noon in the dining hall.

The following Saturday, Touchdown Club Day, the festivities are sponsored by the Cleveland Touchdown Club. They sell box lunches by the thousands, and the people gather under the huge trees to eat mountains of box lunches before going to the stadium for the game about 2:00 P.M.

The small stadium will hold about two thousand people, and there are usually about ten thousand fans present on these days. It's strictly standing room only, and the fans press in along the sidelines and fill the end zones, so the playing field must be roped off. It's a good-natured, jubilant crowd.

We work out in shorts early

On scrimmage day, we work out in shorts about 9:30 A.M. We have our noon meal early, about 11:30, so it will have time to settle before the head-knocking starts at 2:00. We gather in the meeting room about 1:55, and Blanton tells us what we are expected to accomplish. Everybody is dressed in full battle gear. Arm pads are taped on, helmets in hand, ankles taped tight— the smells and sights and sounds of a team ready to do battle.

Blanton always says a word or two about cutting the squad; it must be cut to about fifty players before the exhibition games. As a matter of fact, some cutting is done even before the scrimmage, but the coaches can't tell too much about the rookies until they see them in contact workout at full speed.

It is important to have a game situation and give everybody a chance to play. While it isn't a hard day for the vets, the pressure is on the rookies to show what they have. You can be sure that the rookies don't consider this a festive occasion—it is grueling work.

We go out in units

When we go through the tunnel and out onto the field, it is an exciting moment. The crowd roars just like it does at the biggest games, and, with the crowd pressed in so tight around the playing field, it seems much larger than it actually is. Furthermore, their closeness increases the feeling of excitement. Your heart pounds just like it was a big game. Sometimes you get as nervous for these scrimmages as you do for a game.

When we take to the field, the four units go to different, previously prescribed areas. The defensive line goes to the east part of the north end zone; the offensive line to the west part of the same end zone. The defensive backfield is on the northern portion of the playing field, and the offensive backfield is at the south end of the playing field.

The defensive line, of which I am a part, has quite a time because we want to warm up using the big seven-man sled, and the crowd is so thick that we can barely manage it. There's a constant chatter between players and the crowd. This is about the only time the crowd is ever close enough to talk to in a game situation.

Paul Wiggin, philosopher and comedian

Wig was the most talkative guy on our unit. He always joked with the crowd. "Get your peanuts ready," he'd say, "it's almost feeding time." Sometimes he'd add, "Get some raw meat, these goons have evolved to the point now where they know how to use a knife and fork." The crowd always got a laugh out of Wig.

But the crowd is most impressed by Jim Kanicki when we hit the seven-man sled. We get about a two-yard run and slam into it with a shoulder and forearm. When Jim hits it, the pop sounds like a shotgun. He lifts weights, and his arms and shoulders are huge. His two hundred and seventy-five pounds offer quite an impressive sight.

We play by some strange rules

We have some unusual rules for scoring in these scrimmage games. If the offensive team makes a touchdown, they get the six points as usual. There are no extra points, since all kicking and punting are eliminated. If the defense holds the offense, they get three points. So, if the defense holds twice, it is equal to a touchdown by the offense. Furthermore, the offense gets only three downs, since there's no kicking down. The ball is put on the twenty at the beginning of each offensive series, and if the drive bogs down, the defense gets three points and the ball goes back to the twenty. Probably the game would be a bit more interesting for the spectators with some other rules, but they don't seem to mind at all. In fact, they just eat it up. It's been six months since they've seen any football and they're so hungry for it that anything is all right with them. Besides, the price of admission is cheap—free.

Chuck Heaton, sportswriter for the *Cleveland Plain Dealer*, does the announcing over the public address system. The rookies often feel that they don't get in on enough plays to really show what they can do, and they go back to the dorms in a restless mood—in constant fear of being cut.

All in all the scrimmages are enjoyable, but only if you feel your job is secure.

15

One Man Makes the Difference

Training camp is a place of many emotions and contradictions. You can become both depressed and exhilarated. At one point you are made to feel that you are King Kong and the whole team depends on you. A bit later you may feel that the team could do better without your help. I guess football is just that way and that's why it is easy to get hooked on it.

Collier, the psychologist

I mentioned earlier that Blanton Collier, our head coach, is a psychologist. He has always been sold on the psychology of morale and motivation, and he reads everything he can find in that field. It seems to me that if the most important thing in football is being mentally ready, it shouldn't be left to chance. But this will be discussed in detail in a later chapter.

Let's take a close look at Blanton's techniques for motivation. He will try anything if he really thinks it will help us win. It is quite likely that he'll embarrass you by calling attention to your mistakes in front of the whole group. No one is immune.

But he does this to help you. It's like he says, "You don't start to improve until you're willing to admit your mistakes."

During training camp, he often says, "Well, this may be an exhibition, but a lot of you guys are fighting for your lives. We're going to have to make five cuts by Monday morning." With one breath he makes you feel that you are the most important guy on earth and that the success of the team depends on you. In the next breath he implies that there are three or four rookies that could step right in and do a better job than you're doing, so you better get with it.

One man really can be important if he's good

In 1961 the Philadelphia Eagles had a defensive back named Brookshire who was hurt and laid up for the season. The Eagles had been winning and were sure contenders. But with Brookshire out and a rookie defensive back in his place, they began to fall apart.

It all started with the game against the Giants where Del Shofner, my old buddy from Baylor, was playing split end. Del was one of the truly great receivers, as you know if you watched television the past few years. Brookshire could stay right with him, but Shofner was too much for an inexperienced rookie to handle. The Giants beat the Eagles badly that day, all because one man was out of the line-up. The loss of this one key man and this one key game caused the Eagles to have a bad year instead of winning their division.

Anyway, Nick Skorich was the head coach for the Eagles that year, and because of one man getting hurt, Nick lost his job. But this was fortunate for the Browns, who hired Nick right off, and he's one of the best coaches I have ever played under. He coached our defensive line through the 1967 season, and in 1968 he moved over to the offense.

Mo goes over the detail with the defensive line

Our daily 7:00 P.M. meeting is always held in the big meeting room just off the dining room. Blanton opens the meeting by discussing our progress. He lets us know where we stand, both as a group and as individuals.

Following this, we break up into our offensive and defensive groups. Occasionally, our defensive group will meet together as a unit, but we usually split up into defensive backfield and defensive line units.

When we study as an entire unit, Mo presents a new defensive play and explains carefully and in detail what each lineman and each linebacker does.

Howard Brinker gives us something to look at

Howard Brinker is the head defensive coach. He is a soft-spoken person, but he knows the game as well as any man in football. He's dedicated and a hard worker, but he has a ready smile and is well-liked.

Howard usually works with a movie projector, showing action from last year's games to illustrate the main points of discussion in the meeting. Sometimes he uses an opaque projector in the presentation of mimeographed defenses. From this, we can copy the plays into our books for later study. This part of the meeting is usually concluded with a movie that has been edited from last year's game films to illustrate our success or failure in running a particular defense. We may have used it in every game, and the coaches have gone through many films to pick out the sequences in which that defense appears. The coaches work full time in the off-season, and this is one of the things they do.

We separate into defensive units

Next, Mo works with the line and Howard meets with the backs, and we talk about our specific problems. We learn as much as we can about our specific assignments as individuals relative to the defense we are discussing that night. The next day we'll use the defense on the practice field. By the next night's meeting, we will have seen that particular defense on the screen as it occurred possibly fifty times in fourteen different games, diagrammed it ourselves, heard it discussed by the coaches, and run it in dummy scrimmage. If repetition is the way to learn, then we learn it. It's not enough just to know your assignment; you must be able to do it automatically.

I usually set some private goals to shoot at

I guess the story about Brookshire's getting hurt and the Eagles' having such a bad year, resulting in Nick's getting fired really got to me. I keep thinking about how important each man is to a team even though it takes all of us to win.

Benjamin Franklin had a gimmick for self-improvement. He always listed his goals on a piece of paper, graded himself on how well he accomplished them, and checked them off as he became satisfied with his accomplishments.

There is a great value in thinking big

I follow Ben Franklin's example—I really believe in it and know it works. My goals are listed every week—I write them down in big letters and underline the things I want to accomplish most. Then, I read and study those goals for about thirty minutes every day, letting them sink in, and seeing myself accomplishing them in my imagination.

After writing my goals down, I turn out the lights and concentrate. I see myself doing everything I've just written down. I imagine myself in each situation and visualize how I would react. I convince myself that I'm going to do those things tomorrow or in the exhibition game coming up.

Be specific

In listing my goals, I believe in being specific—stating the number of times I'm going to get to the passer, the number of unassisted tackles I'm going to make, etc. It won't get the job done if I just tell myself that "I'm going to do a better job of rushing the passer today." I must put it down where I can see it, and when I see it I get the feeling I can do it.

Personally, I find it necessary not only to list the number of times I'm going to do a certain thing, but also to list and visualize the number on the jersey of the guy who is going to try to keep me from doing it. I've got to live with that big 76, Bob Skoronski, staring at me on my sheet of paper. My goal is not simply to pin down the opposing lineman, it is specifically to pin down Skoronski.

To improve, you've got to research the opposition

It is very important to research the opposition. I don't do it haphazardly; it must be done carefully and meticulously. One of the things I have learned is not to take chances with my memory, so I write it all down where it can be seen and studied. I study it first with my eyes open, and then I close my eyes and visualize those big tackles making the moves that I know from my research they're going to do. This way, I can pre-condition myself to make the moves that will get me past them and onto their quarterback.

I also watch other defensive ends

I not only study what the offensive tackle I'm playing against may do, but I study what other defensive ends are doing. Incidentally, in studying the opposition it is helpful to study one of the best in the business—for me, this is Willie Davis. Monte Clark, our defensive tackle had this to say about Willie: "He was just all over me—no special move—just all over me and nothing could stop him."

I've also studied Deacon Jones a great deal. He is a great one with a style all his own. He doesn't help me as much, though, because his style is born out of his size and speed. If I tried to play like he does, I wouldn't be very effective, but I have learned some things from him that have helped me.

The coaches set goals too

Don't think for a minute that this matter of goal-setting is a private thing with me. Goal-setting as means for motivating pro football players is practiced regularly by the coaching staffs.

Blanton Collier is a firm believer in setting goals, for both self and team improvement. Blanton says, "Our immediate goal is the game this week and our ultimate goal is the championship." Tom Landry, the Dallas coach, is also a strong believer in goal-setting. I heard him give a helpful lecture at a Fellowship of Christian Athletes retreat on the subject.

Nick Shorich used the same approach in our defensive line meetings (before he switched to coaching the offense). I've heard him say, "All right, we need to get the passer fifty times this year." He then established individual goals for each player. Sometimes before a game he'd come up to me and say, "I want to see you get that passer three times." Then he'd add, "And I want to see you play that short yardage better." He also did the same for all the other defensive linemen.

Coaches have a tough job, because they've got to keep us motivated individually and as a team. Obviously, the best way I can help the team is to do my own job well—the important thing defensively is to "play your own." One of the worst things a defensive lineman can do is to fly off to help someone else when his own job is not taken care of. Each player has a primary and a secondary responsibility on every defense, and if everybody did his own job, few yards would be made on any play. Pursuit is important, but only after your primary job is done.

Players should definitely help each other

On the other hand, some players are interested only in their own play and have no concern for helping their teammates. An outstanding exception was Pete Retzlaff, who played with the Philadelphia Eagles until his retirement in 1966. He was an all around nice guy in every way. When Catfish Smith (now with our team) was playing with the Eagles, he was second string behind Pete. Cat told me, "Pete always made me feel important. We were roommates, and he treated me like an equal. We would discuss how Pete could beat the defensive back he was playing that week. When he'd come out of the game, he'd head straight for me on the bench and ask for suggestions as to how he could play better. I came to know him so well that I felt I could really help him. He's just the greatest!"

When Cat was in the game and Pete was out, Pete did everything he could to help Cat play better. It's the mark of a big man—the way he treats his teammates, especially the guy that might just take over his job.

After all, everyone should share a common goal on Sunday, and that is to be on the top side of the statistic that really counts—the score.

16

Eating Is the Best Part of Training Camp

Chuck Heaton, sportswriter for the *Cleveland Plain Dealer*, says that they ought to change the name from Hiram to Eatin' while the Browns are in training camp. We really do put the food away.

At Hiram College, the cafeteria is snuggled in between Centennial Hall and Booth Hall—two girls' dormitories, one of which is used by the team. Adjoining the cafeteria is our squad meeting room where we have chairs with our names taped to the back. It doubles as a TV room and a projection room for studying films. We enter the cafeteria through this room.

There are always several kinds of soft drinks and juices for us after our workout. We really put the liquids away after our two-a-day workouts in the heat of July and August. The mess hall manager mixes about eighty gallons of lemonade each week, and he says that we drink over two hundred gallons of thirst quenchers of all kinds during a week.

We are served cafeteria style
As a rule, we come down from our rooms early and watch

TV in the meeting room while we wait impatiently for the six o'clock meal. One table is filled with glasses and ice, and most of the guys get two or three glasses. These are filled with tea, lemonade, milk, grape juice, or any one of several brands of soft drinks. The typical tray is filled with a salad bowl, a jello dish, a meat plate, a vegetable dish, and as many tall glasses of liquids as the tray will hold. Gene Hickerson and Monte Clark are usually among the first in the dinner line, and I'm never too far behind.

We really like good food and plenty of it

We eat a lot of soup. Chicken is the favorite soup—about fifty gallons disappear each week. And over one thousand pounds of meat are consumed each week. Roast beef tenderloin is the number one choice, with strip steaks, T-bones, and prime rib roast following in about that order. You've heard of *standing* rib roasts. I never really understood what that meant until I went to training camp. These rib roasts really stand. Some are two feet tall, and the meat servers slice off big chunks of it and toss it on our plates. In addition there are always potatoes, salads, and green peas. Probably, corn on the cob is the favorite vegetable. The cook puts on one hundred and twenty ears each time it is served.

Ice cream is the preferred dessert—eighteen gallons disappear every day. It is smothered with strawberry, chocolate, or butterscotch syrup, and is topped off with ten dozen cookies.

A few guys are calorie counters

With all of this good food around, the weight watchers have a hard time holding it down even though we all work out very hard.

Blanton is pretty severe with the overweight guys. He really gets on them. When the guys complain, he quips, "What you weigh speaks so loud, I can't hear what you say." He goes on, "Gaining weight and not eating is impossible, and don't insult my intelligence by telling me that you aren't eating if you are gaining weight." The football player who gains weight at training camp is the perfect example of the fact that exercise alone won't take off the fat.

The caste system prevails in the cafeteria

There are a dozen or so big round tables in the cafeteria that will accommodate six to eight people each. This is where the caste system shows up again. The coaches and trainers eat together, and the rookies eat separately from the vets. No one says anything about it; it is just understood that way.

I'm sure the coaches follow an unspoken rule which prohibits fraternizing with the players in a social sense; otherwise they would sacrifice the control that they must have to get the best out of them. The coaches do insist that we call them by their first names, and there is a lot more camaraderie between coaches and players than in college. However, there's still not so much familarity that they find it hard to chew you out when they think you need it. The seating arrangement at meals is not accidental. Those who are of the same status tend to sit together.

It's different on the road

At training camp everybody gets as much as he wants to eat with the exception of the overweight guys. On road trips there is a somewhat different system, and occasionally the caste system emerges in a different way. The restaurant owners sometimes cater to the coaches and trainers since they want to keep their business on subsequent road trips.

Some of the players with Philadelphia were telling us about an incident that happened on one of their trips. Floyd Peters got so put out about this that he lost his cool. Floyd got an unusually small piece of meat, and the chunks on the coaches' plates were much bigger. Floyd sat down to eat his, and then suddenly speared it with his fork and, waving it around with gravy flying everywhere, he approached the coaches' table. "Look here what we're supposed to get out there and play ball on," he virtually yelled. "There you guys sit with half a beef while we eat the leftovers."

The coaches were dodging that flying gravy and trying not to create a public spectacle. They finally got Floyd cooled off and quieted down. All of the Eagles had an extra cut of meat from then on. But I don't want to overplay this, because we always go first class and are usually treated better than we deserve.

Heavy on fresh fruit

As we leave the dining room, we pass a table that is heaped with fresh fruit. We are encouraged to take a handful back to our rooms to eat as a bedtime snack. When I was at Detroit, they had a big fruit table and a handy supply of paper sacks that could be filled and taken out.

The "coffee club" provides an opportunity

There are six or eight teen-age girls who work at the dining hall. One night a couple of years ago at the "coffee club" in Garretsville, three of the girls came in and sat down at a large table with Mo, Stan, Monte Clark, and me. They were having a soft drink with us to celebrate our leaving training camp the next day.

Ultimately, the conversation turned to religion. One of the girls claimed to be an agnostic. Possibly, she was just trying to keep the conversation going, but I don't think so. Mo and Stan are Catholics, and they began to tell her that she shouldn't throw everything overboard—that she should "keep the faith." Monte and I chimed in with the same kind of advice from our Protestant backgrounds. It was a very interesting session. Several other people were in the cafe, and everybody listened as we presented the Christian answers to her agnostic feelings. I think she was surprised that all four of us were so strong in our concern for her. Also, I think we had better answers than she thought we would.

I have found this to be the case many times with young agnostics. They seem to think there are no answers to their questions and are quite shocked when they are exposed to a Christian perspective.

17

The West Coast Trip

The start of the exhibition season is always a welcome event. After the long tough grind of two-a-day workouts, we look forward to getting on a plane and seeing what the rest of the world looks like. The ax has fallen for many and the club is down to about fifty. The guys who are left now have a pretty good chance of making the team. Only ten more have to be cut or traded to get down to the forty-man squad. And most of these will be kept on the "taxi squad."

The gala attitude

Morale among the players picks up, but it seems to be a time of increased pressures for the coaches. They get jittery over the possibility that the players will develop too much of the "gala attitude," as Blanton Collier calls it.

In our meeting on the morning of that first exhibition game Blanton will say, "I know this is in exhibition, but I also know the stage is set for us to get the hell kicked out of us!" He so seldom uses swear words of any kind that his use of "hell" is kind of startling. He goes on, "I've seen this drama unfold before. We catch them with tears in their eyes and we're thinking, 'Exhibition, so what?' Know what they're thinking? They're thinking, 'We've got to prove something. We lost the last game by a narrow margin. Big crowd. Home town favorites—win now, or the crowds will leave us.' They're ready for us! Do you hear me? They're just licking their chops and waiting all steamed up to cut down the Cleveland Browns!"

Blanton really gets on his high keys in situations like this. "I want us to win and I don't want anybody hurt. The only way in the world to do that is go out there and give it everything you've got."

We leave the meeting room all charged up, but you can just feel the futility of trying to get the guys really worked up over an exhibition away from home, especially on the West Coast.

Los Angeles

A trip to Los Angeles is sure to be something of a gala occasion no matter what you go there for. I'll grant that it is different when you are going for a championship game such as the Super Bowl. But it's pretty hard to think and live football in Los Angeles one hundred percent of the time. And at this stage, even the coaches don't want you to be too serious.

We usually arrive in Los Angeles on Friday for our first exhibition game. Since the game is played on Saturday, we work out just once. For several years we stayed at the Hollywood Roosevelt Hotel and held our workouts at the Hollywood High School stadium, situated conveniently very near the hotel. But in recent years we have stayed at the Ambassador Hotel and worked out at U.S.C.

The Coliseum

The Los Angeles Coliseum is a good place to play football. The dressing rooms are as good as you'll find anywhere. We enter the field through a huge tunnel that is big enough to drive a trailer truck through. The stadium has been reworked for football, and it seats around seventy thousand. And the field is always in great shape for the first exhibition game.

One of the big attractions of the Los Angeles Rams is their tremendous defensive line—the Fearsome Foursome: Merlin Olsen, Roger Brown, Lamar Lundy, and Deacon Jones. They're probably the best defensive line in the business.

Deacon Jones is one of the best

Deacon Jones is, in my opinion, the best of the four. He plays my position the way I wish I could. I admire and even envy his ability. He is one man in pro football that makes me feel inferior. He's fast and big.

One day after our game against Los Angeles we were on the bus going to the airport to catch our plane to San Francisco. Art Modell, the Cleveland Browns owner, overheard me say that I thought Deacon was just fantastic.

"What might he be doing that we're not?" he asked. Right here the red lights flashed on in my head, because I knew that Art would tell Blanton what I said. Also, I didn't want what I'd said to reflect on our coaches. Finally, I replied, "Well, I don't know. Maybe they play a more gambling type of game."

I do think Deacon is great because he's given more freedom to go inside when he wishes or to take an immediate outside move. He doesn't have to hesitate in order to think through the play and analyze what effect his move is going to have on the team effort. This freedom makes an individual player stand out —sometimes at the expense of the others on the team. If a man plays his assignment to the letter, he isn't likely to make quite as big a splash.

But, Deacon has some great moves—he gets his hands on you quickly and he's agile and strong. And when he guesses wrong, with his speed, he can recover quickly and still get in on the play.

San Francisco

When we play San Francisco, we usually stay at Rickey's Hyatt House (in nearby Palo Alto), and we practice on the Stanford University practice field about five miles away. This is a quaint and interesting place in itself. It is a complex of cabana-style rooms with ten or fifteen rooms in a group and with a park-like area where there are pools, fountains, flower gardens, statues, and grass that looks like a putting green. It's really more like a motel than a hotel, although there is one big high-rise section.

Sunday and Monday are our rest days. We're actually free from the time of arrival in San Francisco about 9:30 Sunday morning until dinner on Monday evening, after which we have our 7:00 o'clock squad meeting.

Monte Clark lives in Redwood City (about twenty minutes from Rickey's) during the off-season. Two or three of us usually visit in his home, and I often speak in his church on Sunday. His pastor is a warm, wonderful person who was a great comfort to Monte and Charlotte when their little four-year-old daughter died of leukemia several years ago. Pastor Dwight Small helped to guide Monte and Charlotte to accept their daughter's death and have a great Christian victory. I have also established a refreshing friendship with Dr. Small and enjoy our lengthy conversations.

San Francisco is "the city everybody loves." It is quaint and picturesque. We always enjoy visiting Fulton Market, Fisherman's Wharf, the Golden Gate Bridge, Chinatown, and many other colorful attractions. During August, when we have our exhibition out there, the weather is always great.

Stanford University, located in beautiful Palo Alto, has an impressive campus, and the drive there by bus is quite scenic. Our Stanford workouts are held every afternoon at three from Tuesday through Saturday.

We get a visit from the head of the officials

As a rule, our stay in San Francisco is punctuated by a visit from Mark Duncan, head of the pro football officials from the

NFL. First he discusses any new rules that were formulated during the off-season. Then, for the benefit of the rookies, he points out the difference between college and pro rules.

Duncan reviews the game rules. He reminds us that the defensive line cannot club opposing tackles in the head. In turn, we remind him about watching the offensive lineman for holding, and then we launch into a discussion of exactly what holding is. He also warns us about not hurting quarterbacks by hitting them after they've thrown the ball. He points out that while we cannot be expected to stop in mid-air, we must not hit the passer after the ball is thrown. Duncan explains that officials are able to see the whole action while a player can see only part.

Life at Rickey's

Our life at Rickey's is a good change of pace. The surroundings are beautiful; the food is good. We follow a set routine: breakfast at 8:30 starts the day, followed by a morning meeting at 9:30. After the meeting, we usually stroll over to the main office to pick up mail or a paper, and read or sit by the pool until lunch. At 2:00 we take the bus to the field for our workout.

Leo Murphy, trainer, and Morrie Kono, equipment manager, always arrive at the Stanford field house a couple of hours early. Leo gives treatment to the injured and tapes ankles. Morrie keeps all the equipment in shape and puts clean equipment in all the lockers.

After workout a few of us spend some time in the weight room. When we have showered and dressed, we head back to Rickey's for dinner at 6:00 and a night meeting at 7:00. There's a good hamburger stand just down the street from Rickey's that is often visited by players after the night meeting. Bed check is at 11:00.

Kezar Stadium is the scene of the battle

Kezar Stadium in San Francisco is one of the most unique

stadiums in the country. While the seating is one of the smallest in the league and the turf isn't always good, the weather is usually perfect. But before long the '49er's will be moving to Candlestick Park, the home of the San Francisco Giants.

You get some queasy feelings in the pit of your stomach when you walk through the long underground tunnel that connects the field house and the playing field. It's small, poorly lighted, and has a dirt floor. There's usually water dripping from the ceiling in a place or two. It is like walking through a huge culvert where the sand has washed in during a heavy rain. It reminds you of the dungeons or the Colosseum in Rome where animals came out of tunnels to devour the Christians.

But once you're in the stadium it's okay, because San Francisco is a beautiful city, and I've never been in Kezar when sea gulls weren't whirling around overhead.

The rain usually lets up by game time

You've probably seen some real mud baths while watching the annual Shrine game on television around the first of the year. But it isn't so bad during the exhibition season. We may get a shower at night or in the early morning, but it usually lets up by game time.

No one seems to want a wet field. It tends to equalize the game, and unless a team is admittedly weak, most players hope for a dry field. I like good traction because I have to do a lot of maneuvering to beat the offensive tackle. It's a decided advantage to him if I can't make sharp, quick moves in my effort to get to the passer. It's also a disadvantage to running backs who have to make quick moves.

Grading system

Since exhibition games are our first crack at outside opposition, they are also our first chance really to evaluate ourselves. In order to assess the performance of individual players in a more precise way, the coaches use a grading system. The grading system tends to motivate the veterans to get back into the groove and the rookies to prove themselves—each by carrying out his own particular responsibilities.

The grading system is meaningful anytime, but it undoubtedly means the most in exhibitions. While the ax has probably fallen for the last time in terms of losing your job, it's still possible to lose your starting position to a rookie or a backup man. But even when you know you can't lose your job, you try to compete against other players in the league in an effort to become the best in the business at your position.

At the next team meeting after the game, the grades are posted, and everyone is anxious to see how he has done. We are graded in the following categories: tackles alone, tackles assisted, tackles missed, tackles on the quarterback, interceptions caused, bat the ball, hurry the throw, and first forces (first man to break through the line and put pressure on the quarterback).

Dick Modzelewski grades the defensive line, Howard Brinker grades the defensive backs, and Ed Ulinski specializes on observing the defensive linebackers.

The week winds up with gift buying

Late in the week there is a scramble to the local shopping centers, because everybody has to get presents for wives and children. When I used to go out to California with Detroit, they'd say you could tell who had the guiltiest consciences by looking at who bought the most presents for their wives. So, some guys stopped buying anything, but, somehow that never seems to work either. Anyway, football players are no different from other visitors to California—we all wind up our stay by shopping for souvenirs.

18

Esprit de Corps

Blanton always emphasizes the importance of loyalty. During the 1966 West Coast trip, Art Modell, the club owner, rented an entire theatre in Los Angeles to show us a premier of the movie, "The Fortune Cookie." This was a Jack Lemmon movie, and the plot revolved around our team. The picture had been filmed the year before in Cleveland, and most of the team had at least a small part in it. Art Modell and Jack Lemmon became close friends as a result of this association, and the whole club enjoyed getting to meet Lemmon and the entire movie company. But, it had been a year since all this excitement.

We had been in training camp a month. There are so many meetings you are required to attend that when an optional meeting is announced, it's not likely to be too well attended. Blanton let us know that although this was an optional meeting, he thought we ought to go out en masse to see the movie at this private showing for our benefit: "As a courtesy to Art. He's gone to a lot of trouble to arrange it." About fifteen out of the fifty guys on our team went, and Blanton told us later that we ought to be ashamed. As far as I was concerned, I was sorry I didn't go, if for no other reason than out of respect for Art. But then on the other hand, it was optional, and I really didn't want to go, and apparently the other guys felt the same way.

We all know, whether Blanton tells us or not, that any recognition we give each other builds our feelings of being a football family.

We do try to keep up with all the players' immediate families, but I've always had trouble keeping all the kids straight. I'll never forget the time I really pulled off the goof of the year. Vince Costello operates a camp for boys out a little ways from Cleveland, and his wife Sally helps him with it. Several years ago Sally was expecting when we left for Texas, our off-season home. When I saw her six months later, my first question, which frankly was designed to show her my interest, was, "When are you expecting the new baby, Sally?"

If looks could have killed me, I'd be dead. "Bill Glass, you idiot, that baby was born three weeks ago!"

There's nothing like winning

I guess the most important thing about esprit de corps is winning. If you win together, the feeling of unity is there, and if you don't, it isn't. The Browns have been consistent winners over the years, and we have developed this spirit. We have a winning tradition, and are convinced that we can win with or without Paul Brown, Jim Brown, Bernie Parrish, or anyone else. Obviously, Green Bay has had this same winning spirit, as have several other clubs. But once you lose it—it's hard to get it back. This spirit is often called momentum. A player and a team must fight hard to keep a winning attitude.

Esprit de corps comes from mutual respect

Team spirit is dependent on the players and everybody else connected with the team having respect for each other. But it isn't enough just to respect each other—it must be demonstrated in every way possible.

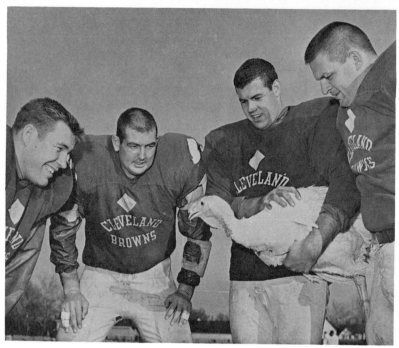

Thanksgiving Day game. Left to right: Bill Glass, Frank Parker, Jim Kanicki, Paul Wiggin.

After the game: Paul Wiggin, Bill Glass, Jim Kanicki.

A snowball fight among members of the Cleveland Browns ended with a broken window. Defensive end Bill Glass, showered with snowballs, looks up at the window.

Bill Glass, Walter Johnson, Paul Wiggin, and Jim Kanicki on Cleveland's snowy practice field.

It is unrealistic to expect pro ball players to be perfect, and you'd be disappointed if you did, but you should expect them to be loyal. And being loyal rules out a spirit of jealousy among the players.

I remember one day we were watching a film in which a rookie defensive tackle on an opposing team made several very good plays. At the break, Vince Costello commented on how good this rookie looked.

Well, in moments such as this, human nature shows through. Frank Parker, who played defensive tackle, said, "He looked all right on two or three plays, but he got blown out a lot. He was trapped once, and he fell for the draw twice. That guard kept him on the line of scrimmage on every passing down."

Vince said, "I saw him on the passer a couple of times, and I thought he played the running game great."

Another defensive tackle came to Parker's defense at this point and said, "Both of those times he got the passer, they were running an X game." (This makes it easier to get the quarterback.)

Vince, who could always come up with some pretty good insights, responded, "You know, I've noticed that no one likes to hear a teammate or the coaches brag on an opposing player in his position. I know I hate like everything to hear them say, 'You ought to watch Butkus or Huff.' " (Dick Butkus and Sam Huff play for the opposition at the same position that Vince played for us—middle linebacker.)

I agreed with Vince, "You aren't kidding. It's natural to hate to hear of other people doing a better job than you are doing in your position." There's usually quick reaction when a teammate starts talking about how great someone else is playing at your position. Maybe your buddy doesn't mean to imply that you aren't doing well there, but many times you can't help but feel that he is.

Criticism helps some, hurts others

Of course, criticism is not a bad thing as long as you are slow to criticize a man on your own team. Team spirit requires you to notice the good jobs your teammates do, comment on them, and go slow on the criticism.

Blanton Collier does this both ways. Like most coaches he'll tell you when you do well, and he's just as quick to tell you when you do poorly. Blanton doesn't usually criticise any player publicly, but he's often complimentary. As I mentioned earlier, he evaluates our play in the squad meetings, and these evaluations are always meaningful to us. But when he says critical things about you in front of your teammates, it makes you want to crawl in a hole. I don't really know how the psychology of criticism works best. It probably varies with different players, so the coach has to decide on a certain course of action depending on the individual situation. I don't think it hurts my play to be criticised in front of the squad, but I'm sure it helps to be praised. Since Blanton doesn't criticise us to the press, he certainly wouldn't want a player to criticise either him or a teammate.

We do read the papers

The general feeling among football players is that newspaper comments really aren't too important. Paul Brown used to say, "Don't pay any attention to the newspapers. All they're good for is to wrap the garbage in." Or he'd say, "Today's newspaper will be the wrapping for tomorrow's garbage." It is still true, though, that all of us read the papers, and they do have some subconscious effect.

I remember one particular write-up in which Paul Wiggin came out really smelling like a rose. Paul was quoted time and time again, and it sounded like the words of a philosopher. He was self-effacing: "On running plays, I've been okay, but to be real honest, I'm not putting enough pressure on the passer. None of us can be satisfied . . ." On and on he went, and he was extremely complimentary of the team: "The best Brown team I've ever been on; I honestly and sincerely believe this." What's more, he handed out bouquets to the coaches, "I like Blanton Collier's attitude. Instead of picking us to pieces when we came in to see the movies Tuesday, he picked us up . . ."

After this particular piece came out, Wig came down to breakfast the next morning and his wife greeted him, "Good morning, Paulyanna."

When he got to workout that day, Vince Costello said, "Paul, that was a great write-up this morning, but don't get the wrong idea—if they could find a rapist that could rush the passer better than you, they'd get him." That's probably an overstatement, but there is great emphasis on results.

They don't always treat me so kindly

We played the Pittsburgh Steelers in a southern city in an exhibition game in 1966. One of the pastors called and asked me to come out and speak to a youth rally. I was hesitant, but I finally agreed if he would promise that nothing would be said in the papers. I usually don't speak on the night before a game, but since this was just an exhibition game, I felt it would be all right. The minister had assured me that "it's just going to be an intimate little group. We'll just advertise it in the church paper. It'll never be mentioned in the local papers." Well, that intimate little group turned out to be a huge crowd.

I spoke to this receptive group of young people and enjoyed it very much. After breakfast the next morning, Mo said, "Man, you really gave the Steelers a boost. They are going to be wild tonight." I just laughed and didn't think anything more about it until somebody else said, "Where did you get your crystal ball?" So, I got a morning paper and the front page headlines read: "Star End Knows Outcome: Browns Have Won Already."

The write-up not only made me look silly, it was filled with plain lies and misquotes. This reporter didn't distort what I said; he just plain lied. I called him and asked, "Why would you say that I said we'd already won, when I didn't even mention the game. And I certainly didn't predict the outcome." He was apologetic and said that he just thought it would make a good story. The pastor knew he was there and asked him not to say anything in the papers about it. The pastor had taped my speech, and I told Blanton and Art I'd be glad to let them listen to the tape to prove that I hadn't said this. They were very understanding.

This was one place where bad publicity had a good effect. It made me so mad that I resolved to tear the Steelers up on the football field. We won.

When a player quits, it usually hurts team spirit

We were all pretty shook up about Jim Brown's quitting the team. But the thing that really hurts is not that some one player does quit, it is a matter of *when* he quits. If a player quits after the team has been built around him, and quits almost at the last day, then it really does hurt.

Jim Brown didn't quit because he was mad or because he thought he was underpaid. Jim had a golden opportunity to become an actor. He had three movie contracts already signed. He could make a great deal more money in the movies even though he was probably making well over $75,000 when he left the Browns. Jim quit at his peak. Unquestionably, he was the greatest running back that ever lived. He was just about thirty and that's not young for a running back. While Jim could have had perhaps two or three more peak years, he was smart to quit when he did.

But where do you go from here? Well, a lot of us were challenged because everybody had said Jim was our whole team. They said we'd be lucky to finish fourth in our division. We agreed with Blanton, "Don't close the casket until we stop breathing." Leroy Kelly took Jim's place and did a great job. The defense played better because "we had to." And the offense was also trying to close the gap caused by Jim's leaving. The main reasons we didn't win the championship the next year after Jim quit were some bad injuries right before a must game against Dallas, and Bernie Parrish's quitting at a bad time.

When a player quits the team, it usually hurts the spirit. This is especially true if a player has a grievance with the coaching staff. Every player has his own circle of intimate friends, so when one guy walks off, he is saying to maybe a half-dozen others, "Hey, you chickens, why don't you show the same kind of guts I'm showing and walk out with me." Usually these intimate friends do stay, but they suffer a morale letdown for several days or several weeks.

Some guys are just unpredictable

You never know what to expect from some fellows—they act so impulsively. Bernie Parrish was like that. He was a great player, but you never knew what he was going to do.

One year, Bernie quit on the first day of training camp. Somehow, you can't blame a man too much for that. Sooner or later everyone thinks strongly of quitting at this time. There you are, faced with a rough three weeks of two-a-day workouts. These are the dog days. It seems you just can't face up to it. I don't think that was it with Bernie—he just decided he wanted to quit.

Then a couple of days later, here came Bernie. He wanted to come back. They let him because he was a valuable player. I'm sure the coaches must have thought long and hard about allowing him back, because in a way it's a bad thing to do. It might encourage more of this walking off and coming back. Anyway, they took Bernie back.

Bernie had a very logical explanation—he's really funny. He said he stayed around the house for a few days and his wife finally got fed up with his being under foot, so she said, "Bernie, you'll just have to get a job." He said, "I went out to look for a job and couldn't find one any better than with the Browns, so I'm back."

Then two years later, in 1966, Bernie quit again. This time

he caught us about three days before the Green Bay game, and he just told the coaches he was fed up and wanted to check out. Again, Blanton said, "If he doesn't want us, we don't want him." So Bernie packed up and went to Houston to play for the Oilers.

We were on the practice field when Bernie finally took off for the last time. As he walked out of the Fleming Field gate, a bunch of us set up a chant. "We want Bernie. We want Bernie. Come back, Bernie. Come back, Bernie." Bernie just waved to us and laughed; he knew we were ribbing him. We did miss him because he was filling a big job, but we didn't want him if he wasn't happy. He had more cause to be unhappy when he left that second time because he was asked to be the swing man for the defensive backs. That meant filling in at any one of the four defensive back positions. He'd always been a starter so I couldn't blame him for being upset. However, one of our defensive backs got hurt that week, and if Bernie had been there to take over, we might have won instead of getting beat by Green Bay by one point (21-20). As it turned out, it just could be that Jim Brown's quitting hurt us less than Bernie Parrish's quitting. Both hurt us!

Friction

One day during a "reading" drill, Jim Kanicki really clobbered Paul Wiggin. We are supposed to run through these drills at about half speed to be sure no one gets hurt. Jim charged and hit near full speed. Knowing Jim, I felt sure that he didn't mean to hit Wig that hard, but Jim is so strong that he doesn't realize how hard he hits.

Wig is normally an even-tempered, friendly, affable guy, but this made him mad. On the next play he charged full speed, and unluckily, his helmet caught Kanicki on the chin, opening up quite a gash. It didn't bleed profusely right away, and Jim stayed in although he was fighting mad.

On the next play, he charged Wig, whose assignment was to

pull away. Jim caught up with him and started pounding Wig with his forearm. There wasn't much damage being done since the blows were falling harmlessly on Wiggin's face mask and helmet. Nick Skorich, our defensive line coach, quickly broke it up, thinking it wasn't important enough to stop the drill—Nick still hadn't seen the gash on Jim's chin.

The next play it was my job to block down on Jim, and I did. He was still so mad that he hit me with a fist in the back of the helmet. I hardly felt it at all, and Jim apologized later. Jim wasn't mad at me, but he was fighting everybody who got in his way.

They had to take seven stitches in Jim's chin. I really thought Wig would be tremendously upset about the whole affair, and he probably was more upset than he showed. The next day Wig told Jim, "I'd like to say I didn't mean to, but I did. On the play before you just plain cheap-shotted me. Of course, I didn't mean to cut your chin, but I did mean to really hit you."

At first Jim didn't take the apology too well, so Wig walked away. Later the same day, Vince Costello talked to Jim and brought him to Wig's room, and there was a complete restoration of relationships and warm feelings. I think they've been closer friends because of it.

Everybody has to let off steam occasionally

It is probably a little surprising to some that grown men would act like this, because it is reminiscent of small boys scrapping. I guess we never really grow up, but there are a great many frustrations in pro football and there has to be some way of letting off steam. It is quite likely that there are adults in your own group who take swipes at one another—maybe not physical swipes, but they cut each other up in little pieces with words.

Players get aggravated with one another for all kinds of reasons, and the coaches are very sensitive about the whole matter of morale. Blanton is a great believer in morale. "We are a football family," he often says. "Loyalty is a must. If you've got some criticisms to make, make them to me and to each other, never to an outsider. I may criticise my wife to her face, but never outside the family."

Christians should be above such things, yet we all slip

One day in a scrimmage a rookie tackle kept holding me. I would break around him for the passer, and he would tackle me. I was getting angrier and angrier. I kept warning him not to hold me, but he just kept hanging on for dear life. Finally, I'd had enough. The next time he grabbed me and was dragging me down, I got ready to give him a good kick. I drew back and started to let fly hard enough to cave in his ribs. But I caught myself just in time to hold up and barely make contact. Everybody saw it, and I was really embarrassed. What a tragedy that a Christian couldn't control himself better than that, I thought. I apologized to the rookie. He graciously accepted my apology and said it didn't hurt, but I was still ashamed of myself.

Alex Karras and John Gordy of the Detroit Lions team were roommates, and they'd get in numerous fights throughout the season in workouts. But they were the best of buddies within minutes after the fights. At times they would even stage fights to liven up workouts. One thing I'm glad of—I've never gotten in a fight during a game. That's where the whole world can see you make a fool of yourself.

Tom Landry believes in closeness through prayer

I was talking to Coach Tom Landry of the Dallas Cowboys while we were in Washington for the President's Prayer Breakfast. He said he didn't know of anything that had developed a closeness among his players as much as having a weekly chapel service. And Tom always leads his team in prayer just before they go onto the field for a game.

Monte Clark told me one day about when he was traded to Dallas on the first day of the season. Tom Landry made an opening statement to the ball club: "Now men, there are three things that I think are very important. The thing that is most important to me is my relationship to Jesus Christ; second, my own family; and third, this ball club. Now, if you cross me in any one of these three areas, you'll have trouble." Monte went on to say that while he was with the Dallas Cowboys he was continually amazed at how true this statement really was. Landry is a man very devoted to his Christ and his family and to his ball club. Every man I have ever talked to about Tom Landry has agreed with what Monte said. This has also been my impression the few times that I have been around Tom Landry. He not only reflects this in an indirect sort of way, but he is also very outspoken about his faith in Christ. Monte says there is nothing that is so thrilling as to see Landry stand before the team and lead the entire group in prayer. He shows equal dedication to the ball club by his untiring labor to make them the best possible team.

Part 5
The Challenge
of Crisis

19

Getting Ready for the Game

TUESDAY, G-5

Preparations begin in earnest on Tuesday for the upcoming game. I call it G-5, because it's five days until game day. We are scheduled to meet our opponents next Sunday in the biggest game of the year. The biggest game of the year is always the one that's coming up. Last week's game is a thing of the past; next week's game is in the future.

Little activity on Monday

Monday is the day of rest for professional football players, but not for the coaches and trainers. The only players who report on Monday are the quarterbacks and any who have injuries. The trainers work all morning on the injured, and the coaches spend some time with the quarterbacks discussing both the game just played and the game coming up. The coaches spend most of their time working on the scouting reports.

Quite a few of us use Monday as a day for speaking engagements. I often have two or more speeches in high school assemblies, football banquets, or church groups. The club man-

149

agement encourages us to make these speeches because it's good public relations. But they prefer that we not do any speaking after Thursday—the closer it gets to the game, the more we should concentrate.

We go to Fleming Field at about 9:45 on Tuesday morning

Players are due at the fieldhouse at 10:00 A.M. on Tuesday, and the fine system makes sure we're on time. We are fined $25.00 for the first fifteen minutes we're late and the same for any part of the next fifteen. So, if you are sixteen minutes late, you'll find your next paycheck will be $50.00 short. Injured players arrive as early as 8:45 to get treatment.

Fleming Field is our new, modern training facility on the Western Reserve University campus in Cleveland. The Browns had it built specifically for this purpose, with a practice field and field house fully equipped for every phase of game preparation. We have showers, a sauna bath, weights, ultrasonic equipment—the works. There is a big meeting room that can be divided into three rooms by folding sound curtains. Each room has a push-button movie screen, movie projectors mounted on rolling tables, and desk chairs for players and coaches.

Immediately adjacent to this big meeting room is the coaches' field house office and dressing room. (They also have offices located in the stadium downtown.) Blanton has a desk in the room, and there's a blackboard on one wall. The other walls are filled with lockers for each of the coaches.

The field was named after Don Fleming

Don Fleming was one of the finest defensive backs that we ever had. He came to play for us in 1959, and was well-liked by his teammates and respected by our opponents. He had a lovely wife named Rosemary and a son named Ty.

During the off-season of 1963, Don was working for a construction company in Florida. He was working on a dragline and was guiding a piece of steel pipe into position by the dragline boom. The boom hit a power line, electrocuting Don.

He was a great favorite on the team and with the fans, so the field was named in his honor. Don Fleming Field is one of the nicest workout facilities in the league.

Getting to work on Tuesday

Most of us live in various suburbs and ride to work in car pools with different ones alternating in doing the driving. Some of the players live close enough to make it to the Western Reserve University campus in fifteen or twenty minutes, but it usually takes me between thirty and forty minutes. We buzz in to practice just after the morning rush hour traffic—down the fast-moving freeways, up through a beautiful park, onto the campus, and into our own private parking lot next to the field house.

Most of the players come rolling into the parking lot between 9:30 and 9:50, but there are always a few who come rushing in at the last moment. Out of the cars, down the sidewalk, through the huge chain-link front gate, and up to the fieldhouse, the players amble in groups of twos and threes. Most of the talk centers around the game just played or the game coming up.

As we enter the door, we are confronted by two, big soft drink machines. Just to our left, there is a coffee urn, and doughnuts are on a small table. Almost everyone stops for coffee and a doughnut before proceeding on past the equipment room and into the locker room. A beautiful, red indoor-outdoor carpet covers the entire dressing room floor.

There's a weight lifting apparatus on one end of the room, and down the center of the room there are rows of large trunks containing extra game and practice uniforms. At the far end of the room is the door to our large training room. It contains tables with cushioned leatherette tops and cabinets filled with medicines and body-healing materials. Vitamins and salt pills are stacked in great quantities on a high shelf at the door. There are several different types of dispensing machines.

Players lounge around in this room and talk about everything in the world. Someone is always running the ultrasonic machine over a hurt arm or leg and someone else is usually under the diathermy machine. Leo Murphy, our trainer, directs all the treatment while chewing on a big cigar. He's usually taping an ankle or knee, rubbing a back or leg, or wrapping a pulled muscle with an Ace bandage. Occasionally, Blanton comes into the training room and the conversation slows down a little while he's there. But the moment he leaves, things start to hum again. He's just nervously checking on the progress of an injured player or checking to see when Leo will be through taping so he can start the meeting.

On Tuesday we dress out in sweats only

We dress in sweat clothes for our Tuesday morning meeting and workout. At about 9:59 Blanton comes to the dressing room door and says, "All right, men." This is his way of calling us to the meeting. Mo perfected the ability to mock him, so he often hides in the shower and bellows, "All right, men." Everybody heads toward the meeting room thinking it is time to start, but then when they discover it is Mo, they turn back to their conversation or to reading their papers to await the real thing.

When the call does come, we head immediately to the bulletin board to see how we were graded on the last game, and from there, we go directly to the meeting room. After Blanton says a few words about last Sunday's game, we draw the sound curtains and meet in our defensive and offensive units to watch the film. They always take a separate defensive and offensive film. We watch only the plays in which we were involved. Our offense seldom sees our defense, and we seldom see them on film.

If you think you did really well, you find that, according to the film, you were much worse than you thought. On the other hand, if you thought that you were just terrible, you are likely to discover that you weren't that bad, after all.

Our coaches are sometimes pretty rough when it comes to calling attention to our mistakes.

Blanton takes over

When everyone is settled in their seats, Blanton begins. The mood of his speech depends on whether we won or lost the previous game. If we won, he's happy and optimistic. If we lost, he usually says, "We could have won it just as easily as we lost it if . . ." or "I told you at the beginning of this season that we could win the championship, and nothing has changed my thinking." Then he tells us that we must develop a plan to get better every day in workout. Or, he may begin some sort of a statistical discussion of what happened in the game: "We had the ball twelve times and lost it twice because of fumbles, once by interception, and three times because of penalty. We kicked field goals three times and scored three touchdowns." Or, "Defensively, I thought we were improved; offensively, we were worse than before" . . . "Some individual players did well, but as a team we stunk out the place." Or, "We were great, but there's one thing about this league, you can't live on yesterday's victories."

We can always be sure of one thing. When Blanton finishes his little speech, it is time to set our sights forward, not backward. Of course, reviewing last week's game has one central purpose: learn from our mistakes and improve for the future. There is a definite break between dwelling on the past and looking to the future. It comes very abruptly when Blanton says, "Okay. Wash that game out of your minds." The implication hangs in the air, whether or not he says it: "You'd better start getting with it right now for the game this coming Sunday."

Most of the time we accept the criticism of the coaches, since it's always meant to be constructive and to help us. However, sometimes there is an explanation by players as to why they did a certain thing on a play. Many statements by players will start like this, "I'm not making an excuse but . . ." Then the coach will reply, "I can see why you were thinking outside on the play, but you must take care of your primary responsibility first, then you can help someone else."

We hit the field running

After the film study is over, we go out for a workout on our own. Most of us start out running. The whole idea is to get the kinks and soreness out. The quarterbacks limber up their throwing arms by passing to the receivers, and the punters boom the ball to the kick return men. It's quite informal and disorganized, with the specialists practicing their specialties, and the rest of us taking laps to get our legs loose or doing a few sprints to insure staying in good shape. I like to run hard early in the week and ease off late in the week, so, I really work hard on Tuesday. Most of the players do. I finish up my workout by catching some passes thrown by one of our quarterbacks or some other teammate. Don't get the wrong impression about all of this energy. I'm a naturally lazy guy, but I just have to force myself to work even if I don't want to. It's a good discipline for me. The longer I play, the more I'm impressed with the unbelievable durability and power of the human body. The most valuable part of physical exercise is that it serves as a psychological discipline.

Blanton always walks around among the players calling one after the other to one side to talk with each about some problem he's having. He will also compliment a player if he did well, but as a rule, he winds up by saying, "I feel you could improve by doing this . . ."

Then sauna, shower, and talk

The sequence is pretty well established for Tuesday after the limbering up workout. First, we go into the sauna, get up a good sweat, and then shower.

Throughout all of this routine, the rhythm and mood of the week is really being set as the players talk among themselves and discuss progress. Coaches can do a lot of coercing and use psychology to try to get players up, but in the long run, it is the interaction among the players themselves that really sets the tone. If things are right for a supreme effort on Sunday, the beginning is felt right here in these bull sessions.

We discuss the players we are going to face next Sunday, the events surrounding the last game we played against them, how badly we want to beat them, how much money it will mean if we go to the Super Bowl, etc.

The team captains are very conscious of the psychology of winning, and they begin early to try to start the ball rolling in the right direction. However, every man is fully aware of the implications of our attitudes for victory. We know that we must avoid "getting high" too soon. It has to be timed just right. If we get too excited on Tuesday, we'll hit a peak about Friday and be on the way down by Sunday. Everybody is conscious of these factors, but above all, we know that if we want to win, we've got to generate a winning attitude.

20

Getting Ready for the Game

WEDNESDAY, G-4 And THURSDAY, G-3

On Wednesday and Thursday mornings we go directly to the full squad meeting in our street clothes, since we do not work out in the morning again until Saturday. It's on Wednesday that you're able to see the scientific methodology of pro football.

Scouting reports

Each of us gets a scouting report on the team we're going to play on Sunday. The coaches have been working hard since early Monday morning to get this ready. The scouting reports are in brown notebooks and on Wednesday these are handed out to us. Each of us takes the report out of his notebook that concerned the team we played last week and replaces it with the new report. The old reports are stacked in boxes, to be resurrected the next time we play that particular team. The new report contains information about the team we are getting ready for, and it is usually about thirty pages long. There is every conceivable kind of information that can be gathered on the opponents we will face on Sunday.

The coaching staff compiles this scouting report by reviewing the last three games our upcoming opponents have played. They gather their information from films of those games, as well as from reports of scouts who saw those games live. Since all of our coaches have been around the league for many years, they also add their knowledge of the history of the opposing team. Many teams now use computers to help analyze the material. The scouting report is unbelievably comprehensive.

The offense and defense get separate reports. We study the opposing offense and our offense studies the opposing defense.

A look at the opposing personnel

There is an in-depth study of every player on the opposing team who has played in their last three games. This report calls attention to the strengths, weaknesses, and prevailing tendencies of these opposing players. It's all there in black and white. If Snowden is to be the opposing tackle, I have a clear report on what Snowden does.

With our scouting reports in hand, we engage in a full discussion of the opposing personnel. First, we see the offensive team flashed on the screen by an opaque projector. Each player is discussed by "Mo," and questions are asked by players. We then study their offensive patterns with the help of diagrams that show their running and passing plays. Their strengths and weaknesses are discussed in detail.

Howard Brinker discusses the offensive pass patterns and suggests the best methods of dealing with them. We are shown their running plays, with special attention given to those which are unique or used most often.

The majority of the teams use certain basic plays with little variation, but there are some unique plays every team uses. Green Bay uses only a very basic offense. They are probably the most predictable in the league. They say in essence, "Now here we come; you try to stop us." Sometimes you can, and sometimes you can't. Dallas, on the other hand, has an offense that is almost completely unpredictable. You can't just dig in and fight the way you would with Green Bay. It's more a matter of staying alert and hanging in there loosely. If you play Dallas the way you would other teams, they trap, draw, and fake you—anything to keep you off balance.

We have a ten-minute break

At this point Howard says, "Take ten." We leave the meeting room and go into the dressing room where Morrie Kono (equipment manager) has sorted the mail that is brought over by a messenger from the office at the stadium downtown. It is sorted into separate stacks for each player. Everybody picks up his mail and either puts it in his locker for future reading or reads it right then.

Some of us like to get another cup of coffee or have a brief treatment with a hot pack. These hot packs are about the size of a baseball base but only half the thickness. They are filled with a liquid that holds heat for about thirty minutes after being taken out of the hot water container. Also, we take our salt tablets or vitamins if we hadn't earlier.

Bernie Parrish and John Morrow used to have private phones in their lockers. Bernie wanted to keep in touch with the stock market and John, with his office (he was in the cardboard box business). They took a lot of ribbing about it at first, but, since the only other phone in the dressing room is a pay phone, everybody was always borrowing theirs. It's too bad both of them are gone now; we're back to one phone again.

More films to watch

Following the break, we are called back in and the meeting proceeds. The second half of that Wednesday meeting is occupied by watching the first of three films we will see of our opponent. If the tackle I'm opposite is a veteran that I have played before, I want to see if he has developed any new tricks. It's also good to refresh your mind on what he's like. On the other hand, if he is new, then you are anxious to study him for weaknesses. If he is a rookie, this is usually a great advantage. Rookie tackles are seldom very effective, because few college teams pass as much as the pros, nor do they use the same style of blocking.

These films help give you proper respect for the opposition. During the showing the coaches keep up a running discussion which is always serious but optimistic. They try to build up confidence by making us feel that *they* have the confidence that we *will* beat them, but they never undersell the opposition. In fact, they usually try to present them to us as being tougher than they really are.

Lunch at local eating places

On Wednesday, Thursday, and Friday the noon lunch is obtained at nearby eating places, or sometimes we bring soup and sack lunches. About twenty of the players rotate in going to a nearby delicatessen for sandwiches. Whoever goes out for the sandwiches pays for them, and then we all chip in and pay him back.

The morning meeting is over by noon and the afternoon workout starts about 1:30. This hour and a half is spent in being taped, having injuries treated, making phone calls, shooting the bull, reading the paper, studying our scouting reports, eating lunch, checking equipment, and dressing for the workout. It's amazing how fast the time goes. There's always plenty to do.

These are the toughest workouts

Workouts for Wednesday and Thursday are the toughest of the week. We start at about 1:30 and work here for an hour and a half. During these two days, we work more as units, running dummy drills on everything. We do a lot of dummy-hitting, using the seven-man sled—hitting and sliding off to hit the next man. We do drills that are designed as attempts to foresee every possible game situation and prepare for it.

The talk goes on

Tension mounts as the week progresses; everybody is using his own techniques of getting himself ready for the big event. But we are saving ourselves for a peak of enthusiasm at game time.

The coaches' lectures get a little longer and more emotional each day. They start trying to find gimmicks to spur us on for this particular game. They discuss humiliating things that happened the last time we played this team, possible injustices that might make us a little mad, every possible reason we might have for wanting to win this big game more than we've ever wanted to win before. Every team we play has some particular way in which they have been a nemesis to us. The coaches and team captains never forget.

You're always a little leery of a team you have humiliated. They're ready to chew you up, and you know it—you can bet their coaches won't forget it and won't let their players forget it.

Films on Thursday

Thursday is the peak day for watching films. The coaches try not to show the same films over and over, but they do try to find different illustrations of what they especially want us to watch. They are also constantly trying to figure out every possible way the opposition could vary their attack or their defense, and get us ready in advance for what might happen. Most teams try some variations early in the game, and the opposition must try to anticipate what that variation is going to be.

21

Getting Ready for the Game

FRIDAY, G-2

All week long Blanton Collier has been anxious about the game, but on Friday he begins to show his excitement even more. He begins the meeting with a speech about the honor of the team, and he concludes it in muted tones about the fact that his reputation as a coach and ours as players is at stake. You know that he is applying psychology and that he is purposefully trying to get you worked up, and yet, you know he's sincere about everything he says. No one doubts his dedication, and no one outworks him.

I can just hear Blanton saying, "I tell you guys that this team is my very life. I've put my life right here into this team. And Art [Art Modell, the club owner] has one up on me. I've just put my life here, Art has put his life and his money on the line.

"This is the game of the year," Blanton will continue. "Either we make it now or we lose it forever." We all know how right he is. Art isn't the only one who has his money at stake, and Blanton isn't the only one who has his life in the game. We all do on both counts. It has gotten to the point now in pro ball that you can earn the equivalent of your full year's salary in just one or two post-season games. How we'd like to make the N.F.L. championship game, both for the money's sake and for the sake of getting at Green Bay again! We are pretty sure that Green Bay is going to be there. We've got a big score to settle with them!

We look at films of our kicking game

We have briefer unit meetings and a shorter lunch period on Friday so we can get back from lunch by one o'clock. At this time we look at the films of our kicking game of the week before. The whole team sees it even though some of us aren't a part of any of the kicking teams. One of the reasons for this is to demonstrate the importance of the kicking game. If a player does well, everybody compliments him and encourages him to do better. If he doesn't do well, he is making a fool of himself in front of everyone.

Few fans seem to realize the importance of the kicking game. A good kicking game gives you field position, but bad kicking coverage not only gives the opposition field position, it gives them points on the scoreboard in a hurry.

There is nothing that will take the wind out of a team like a runback of the kickoff and a seven point lead for the opposition with only one minute of play gone. We spend time on both Friday and Saturday studying the kicking game.

Blanton says that we have three units: the offensive unit, the defensive unit, and the kicking team. Of course, the kicking team is not a fully exclusive team—some offensive and some defensive personnel are used.

It's an unspoken law in pro football that all of the rookies and the non-starting veterans on both the offensive or defensive units had better make the kicking teams. If they don't, they can't possibly carry their share of the load, and they are going to be without a job. But this doesn't mean that the kicking team is made up of the leftovers. Often some of our best players from offense and defense are on these units.

Workout on Friday

Our Friday workouts are lighter in that they last for only an hour. We don't run any contact drills at all for fear someone might get a small injury that he couldn't recover from by Sunday, so we do dummy-scrimmaging at about half-speed. In spite of the light workout, we try to keep the spirit high. The entire team is beginning to feel a little more edgy now as the game is only about forty-eight hours away.

Blanton circulates around. He looks happy one minute and sad the next. We know what it means to him, and we know what it means to everybody.

Friday night is goal-setting night for me

I don't know about the other guys, but I set goals for myself in every game. I write them down, and on Friday night I try to do some visualizing of game situations. If we have played this team before, and if I am sure I will have the same opposing tackle, I sit and visualize the last time I played against him. I see his moves, and I anticipate what I am going to do to counter them. I've been exercising my imagination all week, but as Friday and Saturday come, I do this positive picturing even more intently.

Sometimes I take some films of the opposing teams home with me to get one last look at them. Most of us do this to some degree—the quarterbacks do it more than anyone.

22

Getting Ready for the Game

SATURDAY, G-1

The Saturday before the game, the atmosphere is different. I've often heard teammates say as the tension mounts and the game approaches, "Well, I guess they're going to go through with it." Unlike the space shots, the countdown is never stopped once it starts. There are times that things just haven't seemed right all week and you wish they would postpone the game. But they never do.

Instead of going to Fleming Field, we go to the stadium downtown. We are to be dressed and ready to go on the field at 11:00 A.M. Some of the players bring their children to workout on Saturday morning. My two boys, Billy and Bobby, are always excited about going to the stadium. Monte Clark and his two boys usually ride with us, and we are always in high spirits. The four boys tumble all over the station wagon for twenty-five minutes down the broad freeways, over the high bridge, and downtown into the stadium parking lot. The boys scramble out of the car, wild with excitement; their dads have a relaxed air, but the tension is mounting. The stadium is big and empty today, but tomorrow it will be packed with more than 80,000 people. The television crew are busy setting up for the game.

The boys run off to explore the huge stadium with their shouts echoing through ramps and across the empty seats. Monte and I amble into the dressing room (which is also used by the Cleveland Indians) and dress out in our sweat suits. Then all the Browns gather in the dressing room for another film study before going out on the stadium turf to work out.

Saturday drills

Saturday's film always features the kicking game of the opposition. During practice, the basic patterns used by the opposing team on kickoff and punt returns, as well as their kick-blocking maneuvers, are reviewed for us thoroughly by the coaching staff as they yell, "Run it back," over and over again.

After seeing their kicking game, we review our own kicking game, especially the protection against runbacks. There are several basic things we are drilled on. The field is divided into three sections, with the distance from hash marks to sidelines being two sections, and the distance between the hashmarks in the middle of the field being the third. On protection for returns, there are nine men assigned on the rundown, three for each section. Thus, each man has about a five-yard lane to cover as he goes downfield. The man is responsible for maintaining that lane; if the return man goes up his lane, he'd better tackle him. The remaining two players are safety men.

Protection of kickoff and punt returns is approached scientifically

Nothing is left to chance; everything is planned carefully. On kickoff we expect the ball to go almost to the goal line. We know that the ball will stay in the air about four seconds, and that it will take the ball carrier about two and a half seconds to get the ball back to the twenty-yard line. By running full speed every player should make it from our forty to their twenty in five seconds. Thus, our main force should reach the ball carrier before he gets to the twenty-yard line.

The kickoff man is supposed to be safety on one side of the field and another man, usually a fast back, comes down the other side just in case the ball carrier breaks through the main force of nine men that meet him somewhere inside the twenty.

The nine men are supposed to run as hard as they can to the twenty. Then they are supposed to check their speed and present a solid wall, refusing to let a gap develop in the line, although some lateral movement is necessary to concentrate men at the point of attack of the ball carrier. A pincher situation must obviously develop when the ball carrier makes his cut. Theoretically, you should never have a kickoff returned well, but there is always the possibility that someone won't take care of his lane and there will be a breakthrough.

This would all be very easy if there were no blockers in front of that ball carrier. But there are ten of them, and they are trying to open a hole the ball carrier can break through. So, each defender must control or evade the block and come back into the area the ball carrier is trying to penetrate.

The most effective way to handle the blocker is to fake him out, provided you are still far enough away from the ball carrier and can get back into your lane. If the ball carrier is close behind the blocker, you must keep your feet and control the block while watching the ball carrier; you must wait for him to commit himself.

When you see the ball carrier commit himself, you shed the blocker and make the tackle. Your move must not be made until the ball carrier makes his, otherwise you will miss your tackle. Blanton says, "Football, basically, is like playing tag around a tree. The blocker is the tree, the ball carrier is being chased, and the tackler is trying to tag him. The one who commits himself first is in trouble, but in football the ball carrier has to commit himself sooner or later. So, if you're the tackler, just control your blocker and wait."

The workout on Saturday is short, usually about thirty or forty minutes. Although there are some limited timing drills, we spend most of our time on the kicking game. Dummy drills are run on every phase of the kicking game. Groza always takes a ribbing. If he kicks a long field goal, someone yells, "Good kick, Cockroft!" (Cockroft is the rookie who is trying to take over his job.) The tension has been mounting all week, and a good laugh helps loosen everyone up.

We spend the afternoon leisurely

We usually arrive back home at 12:30 P.M. and watch a college game on TV, trying to relax as best we can. When our game is out of town, we fly to our destination on Saturday afternoon after the morning workout at home. At one time we worked out on the opposing team's field on Saturday, but Blanton changed that a couple of years ago. On the day that he told us about the change, Lou Groza asked, "Coach, is it all right if I shoot home and change after workout?" Ever since, the players have kidded Lou about "shooting home." But many of us do "shoot home" after workout and change clothes (dress suit) and still get out to the airport for lunch.

After a good lunch—salad, hamburger, and strawberry pie—we're off to catch the chartered plane at 2:00 P.M. As a rule, we arrive in the opposing team's city by 4:00 and are met by two chartered buses that get us to the hotel by about 4:30. We either watch TV, read, or nap until dinnertime.

When we are playing at Cleveland, we leave about 5:30 P.M. on Saturday and drive to a downtown hotel where we spend the night. After dinner together we are free to do as we please. There was a time when the entire team was required to attend a movie together, but now it is optional. Some of the players, myself included, just didn't like to go to a movie. I prefer to read, watch television, or review my scouting report again. Some of the time I would go over some material that Paul Wiggin (retired in 1968) gave me every week. This was a summary of

Cleveland stadium. Early morning crowd lines up for ticket sales. Cleveland averages 80,000 attendance at home games.

Veteran Lou Groza, Cleveland Browns.

Paul Wiggin and Bill Glass.

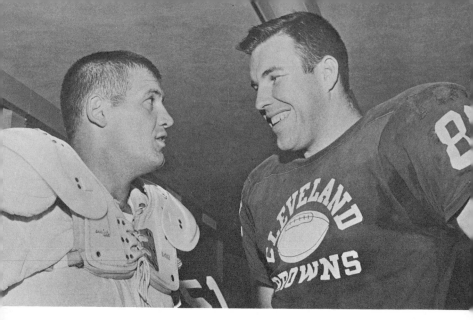

Vince Costello, linebacker, and Bill Glass. Costello was traded to New York in 1967.

Cleveland Browns' veteran defensive ends (left to right), Bill Glass and Paul Wiggin. Wiggin is now on the coaching staff of the San Francisco 49'ers.

the scouting report as it applied to our position. I usually went over to Wig's room. Wig, Vince Costello (his roommate) and I spent the evening talking football. These two guys know as much football as anybody in the game.

Vince was our middle linebacker for ten years. They had tried to replace him every year, because they thought he was too small at two hundred and twenty-seven pounds, but he made up for his size and age with experience and determination. Vince knew the opposition teams like a book—he knew their personnel, their tendencies, their strengths, their weaknesses, and he always had a few ideas about "what they probably will try on us."

Wig was the most affable and knowledgeable player on the team. I could learn more in thirty minutes about the opposing team just by listening to those two guys talk than I could in the whole week by myself.

After a time Vince usually would say, "Bill, let's go to church." So, we would walk down about four or five blocks to a Catholic church where Vince would pray or go to confession. I'd sit in the back and pray or think or read some literature I'd picked up in the tract rack. We'd talk football and Christianity all the way back to the hotel where we'd stop in the coffee shop and have a cup of Sanka. Then it was off to bed, with vows of victory for tomorrow's game. Now Vince is gone (traded to New York) and Wig is coaching at San Francisco, and I'm the only one of that threesome left at Cleveland.

Room check is at 11:00. Ed Ulinski knocks and yells, "Are ya in?" and we reply in the affirmative. By this time I am feeling the pressure. This is for real.

I use positive picturing after the 11:00 P.M. curfew

I concentrate on positive picturing more the night before the game than at any other time. I review the things I've written down early in the week—goals for the game, the traits of my opponent, reminders to myself, etc. A creative and profitable hour is spent just sitting and picturing what I am going to do the next day. I visualize the plays and how I am going to handle them.

The lights are turned out about midnight, and I usually get right off to sleep. I know what I am going to do the next day, and I am ready. The preparation is all over.

But, before I go to sleep, I pray about tomorrow. This is important to me; I know that I need Him in order to do my best. I've got the stuff inside to have a great day, but I need God's help to release this potential. Psychology and physical fitness help, but I need more—I need Him.

23

The Game

After a good night's sleep, I usually wake up around 8:30. This gives me thirty minutes to dress and get down to the chapel service. This service starts 30 minutes before the meal and is led by a local minister. Just about every team in the league has a service like this.

One day we were playing the Eagles in Philadelphia and the Atlanta Braves were playing the Phillies the same day. Felipe Alou and I met in the lobby. I had known him only indirectly before. We have many mutual friends. I asked Felipe if he had time to come up and meet with our group. He consented to do so. I asked him to tell of his conversion, and in his broken English, he had us at the point of tears and then side-splitting laughter over the period of the ten minutes or so that he talked. We parted with a warm handshake and a vow between us to serve the Lord in a greater way through sports.

The rookies and many of the veterans require quite a bit of taping, so they start getting taped as early as 8:00 o'clock on the morning of a game. Since I usually get a light wrap, I slip in about 9:25 and take care of it just before the pregame meal.

The pregame meal comes at 9:30 A.M.

My last meal before the game is fairly light—two eggs, bacon, and about three cups of coffee. In addition, I drink a can of food supplement called Nutriment. It is a high-calorie supplement that gives quick energy. Some of the players eat steak, others eat eggs, some eat both, and some drink only Nutriment.

Everyone is nervous at the pregame meal, and the food doesn't digest well. If you have any tendency to heartburn or upset stomach, you'll have it by 10:00 for sure. I seldom have this problem except right before games. Nick Skorich, really has it worse than I do and is always saying, "Bill, gimme some of your Rolaids."

Most of the guys are talkative at the pregame meal, and the talk is always about the game. I'm usually filled with questions, the answers to which I usually already know, but it relieves the tension to talk about it.

Ryan seems noticeably quieter when under the pressure of game day. Galen Fiss, our captain from 1963 to 1966, used to talk some before a game, but after a game he was so relieved that he chattered like a magpie. He'd talk all night if anyone would stay up and listen. He'd replay the game play by play, and he was seldom complimentary of his own play: "Man, did I get clobbered. Here I was out of position and running like the dickens to try to catch my coverage and wham, out of nowhere, came a pick [illegal block by a receiver]. I was flat on my back looking up seeing stars in the afternoon." On and on he'd rattle. I was always amazed at how he and Vince Costello could seem to remember every detail of the game.

Is the team up?

For years, I've been watching the way teams have acted at pregame meals and during practice the week before, and I can't predict a thing from it. There doesn't seem to be any reliable pattern. If everyone is quiet, it may mean they're determined to win, but, on the other hand, it could mean that they're afraid they're not going to. If they're noisy, it may mean they're taking the game too lightly, or it can also mean they've never been so "up."

Several years ago we were going by bus to Pittsburgh. All of the coaches (except one), the newspaper writer, and the rookies were on the front bus; the veterans were on the back bus with only one coach. Suddenly, somebody threw a wad of paper and hit Lou Groza in the back of the head. One thing led to another and finally the whole bus was involved in a paper-throwing war. At the height of the confusion this one coach, who was trying to maintain some semblance of order, yelled, "All right, you guys are going to get killed tomorrow in the game!" He was promptly plastered by a whole barrage of paper wads.

We won the next day by five or six touchdowns. This is the wildest pregame attitude I've seen a team have. It's hard to tell whether a team is really ready for a game or not.

Unit meetings come at 10:00 A.M.

We assemble in our units at 10:00. The defensive unit is led by Howard Brinker and we go over what the opposing team does on certain formations. Howard draws these formations on the board and tells us the variations they run from each. We've been over this before, but this is a last refresher.

Next, Nick (before he moved to offense) usually makes some comments. He warns us about what he thinks they'll probably do in given situations. Since he's been around the league as a player and coach for over twenty years, he knows the teams better than anyone else. He played for Pittsburgh from 1946 through 1948. It's hard to believe he was an effective guard at 190 pounds. Today, you seldom see a guard under 240.

Ed Ulinski played guard for the Browns during those years and also weighed about 190 pounds. Nick was an assistant coach with Pittsburgh, Green Bay, and Philadelphia. Then in 1961 he became head coach at Philadelphia where he stayed until 1963, when he came to Cleveland to coach our defensive line in 1964.

The bus trip is real quiet

We usually head for the stadium by bus about 11:20. The tension of the past few days is more apparent on the bus trip than anywhere. Everybody is tightened up and nervous. There isn't any jubilation or loud talk at this point, just a feeling of quiet dedication. If the bus is to leave at 11:20 and someone is late, everybody starts yelling, "Let's go. They can catch a cab." Seldom does the bus wait for late arrivals. The coaches are always irritated by tardiness. Blanton says, "It indicates an attitude." After leaving our briefcases in the dressing room, some of us walk out on the turf of the stadium. The crowd has not begun to arrive yet, and it seems to quiet you down just to get a view of the arena where the combat is to take place. On road trips this is a very important thing. There are times when a stadium seems right to you and other times that it doesn't. You're like a speaker who wants to get up and grasp the podium from which he is going to speak and to visualize the crowd that isn't there yet.

I can walk out on the turf at D. C. Stadium when we go to play Washington and get a real lift. We've had some good days there, and I just like that stadium. By way of contrast, Kezar at San Francisco always leaves me cold.

We go out for warm-ups

By 12:50 we are taped and ready to go out on the field for warm-ups. We run in place and do calisthenics, but this is not done in an organized manner. Each of us warms up on his own. During the next stage of the warm-up I work with Dick Shafrath. He practices a fire-out block on me. We hit shoulder pads at pretty near full speed just to get the feel of it. Then I rush the passer a few times on him, and he tries to keep me out of his imaginary backfield.

Following this, the defense lines up against the offense and we have a brief timing drill but without hard contact. During this time, the kickers and other specialists are going through their routines and the quarterbacks are warming up with the receivers catching some easy ones without any defense.

We are back in the dressing room by 1:15

The big test is very close now. We talk to each other and wish each other luck. Blanton calls the squad together and gives us a little pep talk. He is restrained but confident. We really want to win this one.

The coaches, trainers, equipment men, and everybody else leaves the room—only forty players remain. It's almost as if they're saying, "We've done everything we can; it's up to you." The captains take over, and they lay it on the line: "This is the big one." The pressure is terrific. Finally, we say the Lord's Prayer in unison and go out onto the playing field.

Introductions come next

The squad is introduced to the screaming crowd. If we are at home, we can feel the backing the crowd is giving us, and it is exciting and exhilarating. Your pulse keeps pace with the yelling of the crowd, and you just can't wait for that first contact— you know you'll be all right then.

We're behind all the first half

The opposition scores twice on us in the first quarter—we're down 14 to 0. Then, just before the end of the quarter, while rushing Jurgensen, I see he is preparing to release the ball and I leap high in the air; the ball blisters my finger tips at that close range. But the tingling pain feels great. The deflected ball hurdles straight up like a wounded quail hit at close range by a shotgun blast. I move toward the ball to attempt the interception, but Johnny Brewer grabs it and is quickly tackled on their 20-yard line. We score on the first play from scrimmage. It's a great feeling to have a part in setting it up, but we go in at half time down by seven points.

Blanton is hot. He says, "You're playing horrible football."

Sonny Jurgensen, Washington Redskins, tackled by Bill Glass (80).

Jim Brown (32) of the Cleveland Browns scores a touchdown against Washington.

What else can he say, we're behind. We didn't expect him to be sweet about it. The 14 to 7 score was not a true indication of our humiliation—they were beating us much worse than that would indicate.

The third quarter is different

But we go out with a renewed dedication the second half, ready to settle down and pull together.

It isn't long before we are out front 31 to 14. Everything we do is right. Frank Ryan can't miss, and the receivers are great. Our backs are running wild, as our offensive line tears great holes in their line—and, the defense is chewing them up.

Back in the dressing room after the game

It's a happy bunch back in the dressing room. No one is quiet now; everybody congratulates everybody else. "We really lowered the boom, didn't we pal? You played a great game, just great!" Players mill about in the dressing room congratulating each other. There is loud jubilation and backslapping in the training room. The tape cutters zip the tape easily from the ankles, while others are ripping tape off of small protective pads. A player is checking an injury with the trainer. Blanton is checking to see how serious the injuries are. Art Modell is gratefully shaking hands with the players that had a particularly good day. There are soft drinks in a large cooler on one side of the room, and a few players are huddled around it. Then, everyone files into the shower to wash and soap their bruised, dirty, tired bodies.

So it goes week after week. By the time you get back on the bus for the trip to the waiting chartered plane and home, you're already thinking of next week's opponent—the preparation begins all over again.

Conclusion

WHY I PLAY PRO FOOTBALL

So now you have had a glimpse of pro football from the inside. I'm sure I haven't been able to convey adequately the feelings the players have deep down inside. And I'm sure you haven't felt the sting of sweat in your eyes or the sore and aching muscles. But maybe you've seen a little more of what it's really like to be a pro footballer.

It's a rough and tough world in many ways, but it is a world of people—usually *of good people.* They've set goals for their lives and are interested in achieving what they've interpreted to be the destiny of their lives.

I have found a fulfillment in pro football. Somehow, I feel at home there. I'm afraid that it's too often true that we count the fulfillment of our mission in life as a matter of having attained some measure of perfection in a job of one kind or another. There is no doubt that God does want you to be successful as a teacher, mechanic, housewife, or in whatever vocation you choose. But that is not all of it; as a matter of fact, that isn't even the most important thing. Our job as Christians is first and foremost to penetrate the world with a Christian witness.

But this witness that we are to make to the reality of Christ in our lives is not a portrayal of a legalistic religion—we are not to exemplify Christ by a process of negative living, of merely abiding by the "thou shalt nots." Ours is to be a positive, happy outpouring of the love which begins in God and cannot be contained within us since it overflows. If our lives are happy, pulsing with the desire to live fully, with relish and with gusto, then Christianity will be an experience in living that will cause others to want to know our Christ. If our witness is negative and legalistic, then no one is going to desire our way of life.

There is a difference between a life lived legalistically and one lived through experiencing Christ and *then* following Him. It is the difference between living life to its fullest because we love Christ, and living life dutifully because we feel we must or else. You can't be happy doing things because you *have* to in order to satisfy some despot. But you can be happy doing almost the same things because you realize they are best for you.

I have chosen pro football as a profession for these years of my life because I believe that I can become what God intended me to be more fully in pro football than anywhere else. I believe He wants me to share my faith with people everywhere. What better platform could there be than that of the NFL.

I *know* pro football has given me entry into the lives of thousands of people, young and old alike. I thank God for the opportunity to use pro football to His glory and be involved in a great cause in the world.

Epilogue

In the first century sports played an important role in Christian witness. While sports didn't produce Christianity, it did expose Christian strength, faith, and character to the pagan world. They were martyred by the thousands in jammed Roman arenas, and those crowds could neither explain nor forget the victorious manner in which the Christians faced death.

Today, in a world that is splitting apart in a thousand directions because of misunderstanding and prejudice, rebellion, and revolution, sports can be one of the best platforms from which to communicate the Christian solution.

Crowds are jamming the stadiums today like they were in the first century. Athletes are idolized, and they are beginning to realize the awesome influence this gives them. It can be for Christ's sake as it was with the Christians two thousand years ago, or it can be used for selfish motives.

There is a greater challenge than blocking or tackling on the field—it is the challenge of using properly the witness that pro football offers.

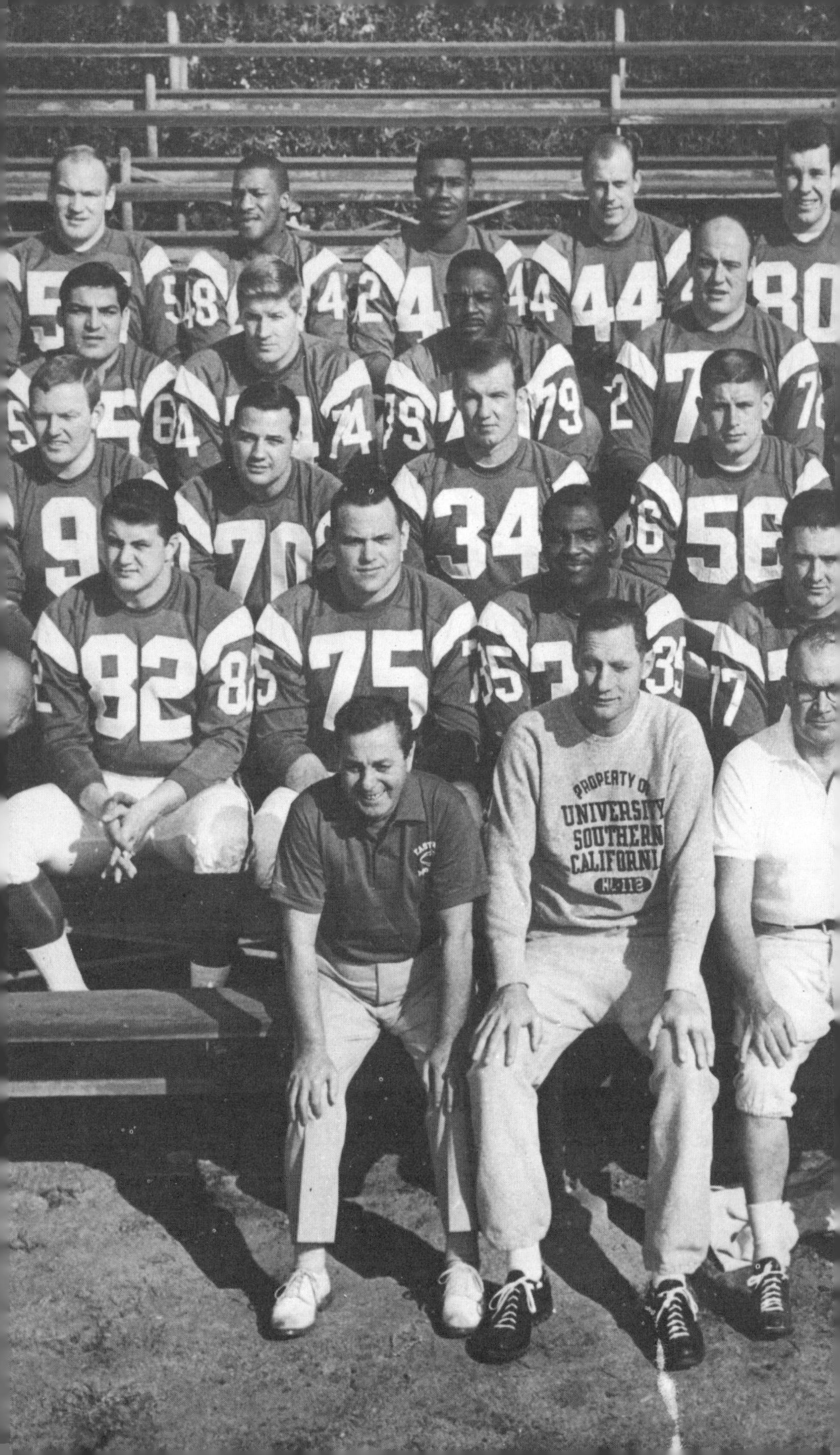
PROPERTY OF
UNIVERSITY
SOUTHERN
CALIFORNI